Energy and
Eros ❧

Energy and Eros

Teachings on the Art of Love

James N. Powell

WILLIAM MORROW AND COMPANY, INC.
New York

Library of Congress Cataloging in Publication Data

Powell, James Newton.
Energy and eros.

Includes index.
1. Erotica. I. Title.
HQ460.P69   1985   306.7   84-27175
ISBN 0-688-02811-X

Printed in the United States of America

First Edition

1 2 3 4 5 6 7 8 9 10

BOOK DESIGN BY BERNARD SCHLEIFER

To Anne

Contents

7

In the beginner's mind there are many possibilities, but in the expert's there are few.

—SHUNRYU SUZUKI in
Zen Mind Beginner's Mind

The Ingénue

*M*ANY OF THOSE who had the good fortune of hearing the late Alan Watts deliver a talk will remember him as a charming, philosophical clown, brimming with humorous insights on almost any subject and displaying his most penetrating wit in presenting Asian thought to Western audiences. On one such occasion he commented on the meaning of the famous Indian incantation, or *mantra*, AUM. In India volumes have been written on this *mantra*, full of abstruse theological flights. One interpretation informs us that the "A" is the waking state of consciousness, the "U" is the dream state, and the "M" is dreamless sleep. When the *mantra* is intoned mentally—AUM AUM AUM AUM—the deepening silence between any two repetitions is the self-luminous fourth state of pure consciousness.

Watts, however, was especially fond of poking fun at the Hindus, and had another way of looking at AUM. When people are young and innocent, he jested, they say "AH!" When they have been around a little while, they start cooing a sensuous "UUUU," and it is only in the wisdom of their golden years that they begin to hum an all-knowing "MMMMM." The secret of life, he added, is to continue feeling the Ah! even while Uuuhing and Mmmming. In other words, don't let sensuous experience or accumulated wisdom over-shadow your simple sense of wonder.

The Hindus believe that the entire creation shines forth from the radiantly beautiful Goddess of Speech. "Ah" is her womb, the primal field of creative energy, innocently giving birth to every sound and form. And if you slowly close your lips while pronouncing a sustained "Ahhh . . . ," you will see how the whole sound of AUM emerges from the "Ah."

The Japanese have an expression for innocence—they call it *mono no aware*—and it means a feeling for the Ah!-ness of things. This sentiment is, in fact, one of the cornerstones of traditional Japanese culture. It lies at the basis of such Zen-inspired arts as painting, calligraphy, music, tea, flower arrangement, and poetry—all of which depend upon cultivating a certain vulnerability to the controlled accident. Thus *mono no aware* has inspired a cult of innocence that makes Blake's musings on the subject pale in comparison. Ah-ness, for Japanese poets, has many subtle shades. It can mean a simple appreciation of natural beauty as when spying among peach trees the first cherry blossoms, or seeing them scattered on the ground like newly fallen snow. Or Ah-ness can contain humor, as when during a sudden downpour, dark thunderclouds crack and ducks scurry about the yard, quacking. It can be almost mysteriously surreal, as when the sea darkens before a storm with the cries of distant gulls, faintly white. It always represents the unexpected, a momentary flash of aesthetic arrest, a nonintellectual appreciation unclouded by previous experience. The sudden snapping of a twig, or the

GONG of the evening bell, bring the awareness intensely into the present.

A few years ago I met a sensitive and beautiful young woman who possessed this quality of Ah-ness to a considerable degree. She had a lively air, an open, oval face, large dark Modigliani eyes, lithe limbs, and an effortless, willowy grace. We became intimate friends, and would often go together for long walks in the woods, delighting in the natural beauty. After knowing each other for some time, she confided to me that she had no experience in matters of love, and wished me to initiate her into its mysteries.

We soon found ourselves alone in a rustic cabin, listening to a recording of a Chopin Nocturne. I began to stroke her dark hair and kiss her. Feeling timid about what was sure to follow, she interrupted, saying, "Let's just lie here and hug awhile, like sister and brother." At that point she put her arms around me and drew me close to her. We began to relax and enjoy the warmth and intimacy of each other's presence, forgetting completely about sex and seduction. After some time I noticed that our breathing had become spontaneously synchronized and very refined. We seemed to be afloat in a sea of tender feeling, falling deeper and deeper into a peaceful but passionate state of repose. Often the boundaries of our bodies simply melted away, our breathing halted momentarily, and we found ourselves merging into one timeless and boundless being. Then our bodies began to shake and quiver all over delightfully, and again we felt the silent, delicious energy moving in us. We lay together for hours this way, exchanging tender and subtle caresses, then falling back into a state of luminous oneness. We had forgotten completely about sex, seduction, virginity, performance, and stimulation, and had simply surrendered to the immensely beautiful waves of energy and emotion welling up within and between us. And so it was that I, who was supposed to be all-knowing in the art of love, was initiated by a young virgin who knew absolutely nothing about sex into depths of artless abandon I had never previously enjoyed.

From then on, I always made certain that our periods of physical intimacy began with a silent and prolonged merging of our beings. Many times it seemed as if all our sensuous, mental, and even emotional faculties were suspended and we were simply soul touching soul. Any movements our bodies made in love were not willed but arose spontaneously like waves in a field of energy. In later reflections I was reminded of the soaring peaks in Chinese landscape painting rising out of the bright, misty void, and of the Taoist strategy of yielding to this all-embracing silence. The Taoists were aware that the deeper and vaster the field we contact, the greater will be our capacity for relationship. As Lao Tzu advised some two thousand years ago, "If you want to acquire the positive, embrace the negative." Embrace Ah-ness, suppleness, and simplicity; yield the private efforts of the ego to the vast relational power of the deepest energy field. "The way to do," he adds, "is to be."

In light of these experiences and reflections, I began to reconsider all the sexual attitudes I had absorbed so unquestioningly as a member of our culture. I also began considering the sexual traditions of other cultures and found that many had discovered a form of communion similar to the one the young woman and I had experienced. This led me to the realization that there are basically two modes of sex. In the West, sex is something similar to eating popcorn. It is almost percussive, requiring sustained muscular activity, and part of the fun is the pressure and the crunch. For lovers of this school, a more contemplative, quiet union would be just like letting popcorn melt in your mouth, and feeling it get soggy until your saliva dissolves it. It misses the point.

In some other cultures, sex is more like eating ice cream. Although to the uninitiated a scoop of ice cream may seem a cold, insipid thing, it contains hidden depths. Compared with the active muscular work needed to masticate a mouthful of popcorn, enjoying ice cream is an act of surrender capable of opening up dizzy heights of aesthetic pleasure—some would even say spiritual rapture. Eating ice cream transcends mere oral gratification, for it does not require the localized effort of only one bodily organ. It does not require jawing, the active engagement of muscle, tendon, and bone. A truly passionate ice-cream eater does not merely bite off a piece with the teeth, but kisses off a lump of congealed joy, sucks the mass tenderly, and cradles it softly between the tongue and palate, allowing its sweetness to fill the mouth, permeate the head, and flow in streams, infiltrating every pore of the being and particle of the spirit. A gregarious chewer simply misses the point.

The popcorn-type lover will most probably be fond of dogs—as pets—requiring the type of panting, drooling affection that only an overeager canine can deliver. Lovers of this school can be classified as Panters, and lean decidedly toward what we might call the Pant Pole of the sexual continuum. Ice cream-type lovers, on the other hand, are more feline in their affections, preferring the sort of wanton purring and supple abandon of a female jaguar cuddling with her mate. These lovers can be classified as Purrers and lean toward the Purr Pole of the sexual continuum. Whatever their inclinations, most lovers are neither 100 percent canine nor feline in their affections, but enjoy a kind of sex that involves both ardent panting and downy purring, avid crunch and silken surrender—something like rocky road ice cream.

Western lovers tend to lean toward the Pant Pole, and subscribe to what might be called the Pant Principle of sexuality. The reasons for this are complex and deeply rooted in our culture, our minds, our hearts, our bodies, and our relationships. The Purr Principle of sexuality, however, has much to recommend it. To appreciate it fully, we must reconsider and free ourselves from our present sexual conditioning. And we must do so not only mentally, intellectually, but also emotionally, bodily, and relationally.

We begin with a reconsideration of sexuality in the West, then turn to ancient China and India—cultures in which the Purr Principle achieved an extraordinary degree of refinement.

Courtesy

*H*E IS HURTING HER. He doesn't know it, of course. In fact, he is pretty sure by the look on her face that she is experiencing the most satisfying of sensations. He can't ask how she feels. After all, he is the man. He is supposed to know.

She can't just scream, "Jesus Christ! Cut it out!" She doesn't want to hurt his feelings. And after all, he is the man. He is supposed to know. Maybe it is supposed to hurt. One thing is certain. She can't say anything. If she does, she will not seem pure and virginal.

Suddenly she knows it is over. She can tell by the grin on his face and by the fact that he has stopped. She says that she should probably be getting home now. He is very courteous. He drives her home, opens the car door for her, and walks her to the front porch. They kiss good night. She goes inside, proceeds straight to the bathroom, and cleanses herself. Next she goes to the kitchen, opens the refrigerator, takes out an entire apple pie, and devours it. Then she retires to her bedroom and finishes reading a romantic novel. He drives down to the gym and brags about his latest conquest.

Meanwhile, on an island in the South Pacific, a young man of thirteen undergoes a ritual that marks the beginning of his sexual experience. The men of his village cut a shallow slit along the top length of his penis. Now the mystery of genital bleeding, previously associated only with women, menstruation, and the miraculous feminine power of birth, is transferred to the vaginalike wound in his penis. Through mimicking the power of woman he becomes a man. A few days later the scab on his penis is still not quite healed, yet he will now make love for the first time. He sleeps with an older, experienced woman selected by his elders. She instructs him that the wound on his penis is still tender, and in order to avoid the pain of tearing it open, he should insert it gently, and only after she is thoroughly moist. Then he must not thrust in and out, but press and rub his pubic area against hers. In this manner he can delay his orgasm indefinitely while providing her with the clitoral stimulation she requires. She then instructs him in a number of positions and imparts a thorough knowledge of female anatomy.

Once initiated, young men no longer sleep with their families but in bachelor huts. A young woman may select a young man and sleep with him in his bachelor's hut every night for about six months. Then she will pick another and spend six months with him. After she has known four or five men in this way, she will choose her favorite and they will marry.

In the Brazilian wilds, night approaches. A small tribe of bush people builds a fire. After eating, couples wander off into the brush to share intimacies. They are often followed, however, by a cheering crowd of onlookers who treat the event like a spectator sport.

By morning all the members of the tribe form one big heap of nude bodies surrounding the dying embers of the fire. This pattern of communal sleeping is followed every night.

The Grand Valley Dani of Indonesia have long puzzled anthropologists. When a couple weds they have intercourse on their wedding night, but wait two years before making love again. After giving birth to a living child, they then abstain from sex for four to six years. Yet such abstinence is endured without signs of unhappiness, frustration, or stress. They appear to be a serene and healthy people.

Since the Middle Ages, various Christian sects in the Soviet Union and Europe have practiced self-castration. They feel this is the only way to overcome the temptations of the flesh. Naturally, they feel that they are the only true Christians.

Humans experience much greater diversity in the forms of sexual life than do most other animals, since within each species sexual patterns tend to be strictly defined. For instance, one variety of shrimp is a type of hermaphrodite. When half grown the shrimp changes slowly from male to female. His testes shrivel away to be replaced by ovaries. When female, the shrimp produces eggs, and while male, he fertilizes them. This pattern cannot be altered—for the life of him/her. Mammals tend to copulate only when the females are in heat. During the off season, both males and females masturbate. Elephants do so with their trunks. As the female approaches heat, she chooses a bull and leads him coyly in a love chase she somehow always manages to lose. Then they caress each other lovingly with their trunks, inserting them into each other's mouths and intertwining them in intricate embraces. This courtship stage lingers for weeks, and when the period of heat finally arrives, the elephants find a secluded bower in which to consummate their relationship. The bull then mounts the cow and copulates without moving his powerful body. It seems that the physics of passion between twelve-thousand-pound creatures has dictated that the male evolve a penis that moves independently of his body. This may help explain why elephants have evolved such long trunks. Once the female becomes pregnant, the gestation period is almost two years. After giving birth, it will be another three years before she comes into heat and is approached again by the bull.

Although female elephants court and mate with only one male, when a female chimpanzee comes into heat, she copulates in turn with every male in the band for ten days on end. Yet she is never considered nymphomaniacal. Her behavior is simply par for the course. Many of the other female chimpanzees behave in exactly the same manner.

In every instance the behavior of animals is at least partially dictated by heredity, though among humans, and perhaps some animals, this inheritance may be as much cultural as genetic. Sex is learned; and what we learn is not without distinct advantages. We are, for instance, almost the only creatures in the entire animal kingdom (gorillas and whales are among the few exceptions) that assume more than one sexual posture. We share with gibbons and dolphins the freedom of not being limited to intercourse only during female-heat cycles. We are virtually the only species that engages in foreplay.

Among humans, then, sexual behavior does not just happen naturally but is culturally transmitted. All our culturally received sexual thoughts, myths, and attitudes constitute what can be called *sexuality. And the physical reality of sex does not exist for us apart from our sexuality.* Although our culture is saturated with sexual advertising, romantic songs, novels, movies, and an endless array of sex manuals, sex itself seems to remain an ever-elusive reality. The more sexuality we produce, the more we talk, write, read and think *about* sex, the more it seems to withhold some as yet undisclosed secret. Only when the latest secret has been discovered in some laboratory, published in a sex manual, broadcast on talk shows, and received as common knowledge, only when that secret becomes sexuality, does it become translated into sex, into what people do in their bedrooms.

Yet if our culture constantly expands the realm of sexuality, and thus actual sexual behavior, has it really increased our enjoyment of sex? Received wisdom tells us that a satisfying sexual relationship is fundamental to a happy marriage. However, only our divorce rate seems able to keep pace with our increasing knowledge of sex. Obviously there is something that our culture is not telling us, or that in telling us, leaves us more confused than when we began. Much of the problem is that conflicts are built into our learned sexual attitudes. Females especially have received the most mixed messages. Many have learned that sex and their genitals are unclean, yet it and they are the ultimate gifts to their husbands on their wedding night. They are expected to be pure and virtuous, yet be good lovers. In short, they must be both virgins and whores. Many women do not know whether it is more neurotic to be innocently chaste or seductively alluring. If a young woman doesn't "go all the way," she may be considered a tease. If she does, she may be called a slut. While sex may be a way to catch a man, an adolescent woman can go only so far if she is not to lose her boyfriend's respect. He is supposed to "go for it." She is supposed to try to disregard her body while yielding precisely enough erotic territory to keep his interest. She must learn the difficult art of inhabiting that exciting space somewhere between strategic submission and adroit evasion, feigned reluctance and fawning surrender. If a young woman behaves in this way for a number of years, it is no wonder that she may suffer sexual difficulties in married life and look back on the fear and yearning of backseat petting as her most highly charged sexual encounter.

Suppose a young woman wants to remain a virgin until marriage. She may prostitute every orifice in her body, with the exception of her vagina, and still stand before the altar with hymen intact. Or she may never kiss a man but become overpowered by a drunken football hero at a college fraternity party. She then carries a triple stigma: She is a rape victim, a nonvirgin, and an inexperienced lover.

Men, on the other hand, don't have it much better. They are supposed to know everything despite differences in male/female anatomy and the individual touching preferences of every sexually unique woman. Yet if they talk with their partners about sex they risk appearing unmasculine. With women, there is an unspoken myth that "if this is true love, he will know how to please me." If he doesn't, and they don't communicate, they both may seek "true love" elsewhere.

So it is that many perfectly good relationships fall victim to culturally transmitted sexual myths. Sex suffers on account of our sexuality. If we are to reclaim an unconditioned sexual awareness, we must review the history of our passions. We must dig down and examine the hidden, silent mythical foundations of our sexuality until finally, like discovering the ageless stone face of some forgotten temple deity, we expose the forces that compel us to love as we do. For by mythical we do not mean unreal or illusory. On the contrary, the mythical is only too real. The myths dictate our every action. We do not think or dream them; they think and dream us. They are so tacit that they defy easy identification, compelling us without our knowledge or consent. We act out the myths as if they were the only reality. They become our very flesh and emotions. Yet if our myths are in conflict with each other, our flesh and emotions must be in conflict also as they attempt to embody the strategies that trouble our sleep. Let us therefore examine this sexual mythology to see face to face the silent commands it urges us to fulfill.

The Devil's Door

Power always seeks to control sex, and one of the dominant powers molding sexuality in the West has been Christianity. It has never failed to inform us of the evil nature of passion and has given us the notion of original sin. Theology being the work of males, original sin has been attributed to females. Jesus was reportedly kind to harlots who displayed true faith. He is better remembered, however, for his statement that "whosoever looketh on a woman to lust after her hath committed adultery with her already in his heart."

Paul of Tarsus took things still further. Entirely committed to Christ and expecting Him to return to earth at any moment, he shunned anything that might interfere with a perfect union between a man and his

Savior—especially a woman. Therefore, Paul lived a life of strict celibacy, advising others to abide in the same manner, stating that "it is good for a man not to touch a woman." He believed that women were inferior to men. For while men were created in God's image, women were created for the use of man and should live in subjection to him. After all, it was Eve who led Adam astray in the Garden of Eden, thus condemning all humanity to the Fall. God had to sacrifice His only Son to redeem the world from this female-inspired state of sinfulness. One wonders why He didn't incarnate and sacrifice His only Daughter.

For those who simply could not love without sex, Paul permitted marriage, advising that "it is better to marry than to burn." Yet even married sex should be only for the sake of procreation, he advised, and devoid of pleasure and passion. There were men in the early Church who "kept a virgin," yet did not marry or have sexual relations. There were many "spiritual loves" during this period, and even Paul could not escape being the object of such a spiritual passion. It seems that Thecla, a beautiful young virgin, was about to be married. But sitting on her balcony one day, she heard Paul delivering a public sermon. Deeply touched by his words, Thecla dressed in boy's clothing, slipped away from her home, and followed him wherever he went. When Paul died she entered a cave in the mountains, where she lived for another seventy years. Eventually the practice of "taking to oneself a virgin" became so prevalent that it was condemned by St. John Chrysostom, St. Gregory of Nazionzus, and St. Jerome. In these relationships men lived with Christian virgins, sometimes sleeping with them, but avoiding orgasm. The Church's objections to these unions centered around the fact that (1) the individuals were not married and (2) their physical intimacy produced no offspring—the only "approved" reason for physical intimacy. Although repressed by the powerful Church, this type of chaste love would surface again in twelfth-century Europe in the form of courtly love.

As Christianity spread through medieval Europe, entire populations came under its dominion, subjecting them to ecclesiastical notions of spirit versus flesh. It provided the symbol that epitomizes the Middle Ages—the rose. As a spiritual symbol, the rose is the Virgin, through which the Lord seeped fragrantly into our world as through the pores of rose petals, spilling their red perfume. Each day as the sun rose in medieval Europe, its rays would stream through the stained-glass windows of French cathedrals, pouring down on pious worshipers counting their rosaries, and illuminating one of the most resplendent architectural motifs of the period. The huge round rose windows depicted the Virgin presiding in the center amid an adoring host of angels, and of doves symbolizing her endowments. Dante beheld the host of Paradise in the form of a celestially pure rose. Angels, the rose's petals, flew up from it like a swarm of bees to the place where the fragrant Light of God abided. Yet this vision was granted to the poet through his ecstatic contemplation of the beauty of an earthly woman. The rose, then, is not all virginal fragrance. The fleshy and dark abyss of its petals was a frank symbol of passion, of the youthful, freshly glowing beauty of an earthly woman. And if the Church could not make room for the innocent love of such beauty, it could only spawn a heresy.

The degree to which medieval life was saturated with Christian dogma is difficult for us to imagine, for every aspect of life was arranged according to a concept of the universe that the Christians had borrowed from the ancient Greeks. According to this geocentric model, the earth is a sphere encased within seven transparent revolving spheres, each inhabited by a planet: the moon, Mercury, Venus, the sun, Mars, Jupiter, and Saturn. The seven days of the week each claim a planet as do the seven metals, the seven tones of the musical scale, and the seven branches of learning. Hovering far above all is God in Heaven. As the soul incarnates, it takes on the quality and element associated with each sphere it passes through, finally arriving on earth. When it returns to Heaven, resuming its virginal purity, the soul leaves the flesh and all its gross elements behind. Thus, the fragrance of divinity is infinitely removed from the dark petals of earthly passion.

The social and religious domains of life were perfect replicas of this structure—the Emperor and the Pope were but the earthly appointees of God. By blind obedience to their decrees one would align oneself with the celestial harmonies and be assured of salvation. The amount of capital and labor invested to reinforce the cult of the Virgin Mother was enormous. For instance, in France alone between 1170 and 1270, eighty cathedrals and five hundred churches were constructed at a cost of some five thousand million francs. However, such a vision of Heaven, the Virgin Mother, and God could hardly have been imagined without the opposing idea of another force. This, of course, was the Devil, who corrupts, deceives, and destroys the soul, dragging it down to another world—a bottomless Hell where it burns eternally.

Heretics in the Middle Ages were tortured and

hanged, yet it was not the rack or the gallows they feared but the foul-smelling flames of the Devil's prison. It was this putrid nightmare of eternal fire that blossomed on the same branch as the cult of the Virgin. Hell was the ultimate destination of the lustful soul, and Heaven the eternal abode of the Undefiled Virgin and her chaste devotees.

In the courts of medieval Europe marriage, though sanctified by the Church, was almost never happy. One married for political or economic purposes, according to the wishes of one's family. Young women hardly out of girlhood were betrothed to much older men, and were often fitted with iron chastity girdles to save them from mortal sin while their husbands were out waging holy war. Should a young woman fall into adultery, she and her lover would face torture not only on this earth but in the ever more intensely feared world of Hell. Thus Church father Tertullian called woman *janua diaboli,* the Devil's Door.

Cortezia

If a young maiden married the lord of a feudal castle, she naturally became the lady of the court, surrounded by her damsels. Yet the males—nobles, knights, dandies, squires, and pages—far outnumbered the women. And all were socially inferior to Her Ladyship. In contrast to the barbarous environment of the surrounding countryside, the lady of the castle moved in a world of charm, leisure, and luxurious refinement. If the union of the lord and his lady was loveless, as it so often was, we can imagine the furtive glances that must have passed between many a troubadour or knight and his coy lady, and the love that must have burned in their hearts more fiercely than the fear of the flames of Hell.

What were they to do?

What they did was to learn a lesson from the East, but in so doing, they created something uniquely Western. Just as it was in Europe of the Middle Ages, at the same period marriage in India was often a loveless one arranged by one's families. In order to make this obligation bearable, the emotion of passionate rapture was channeled toward divinity. Thus we learn from India's sages that there are five degrees of love of God, ranging from the "churchgoing" variety to the throes of divine seizure.

The first type of divine love is like the dutiful relationship of servant to master, so blindly accepted by those wanting to abandon personal responsibility for action. The second stage of divine love resembles the relationship between friends. A servant cannot converse with, question, or argue with his or her master. But true friends accept each other fully and are able to discuss and even dispute an issue openly. Next, we find the quality of divine love between parent and child. Here the worshiper is the parent and the divinity is loved as a child. The fourth degree of divine love is like the love between man and wife, or like the emotion of a Catholic nun who becomes the spiritual bride of Christ. In India it is said that the wife is to treat her husband as a God, and that any household in which women are not treated as Goddesses will not yield spiritual fruit. Thus, even if a husband were a serious yogi yet treated his wife ignobly, his spiritual devotions would be of no benefit. This regard of spouses for one another is a duty and has nothing to do with romantic love as we experience it in the West. Yet the Hindus recognized the importance of passionate abandon, and thus the fifth and highest attitude of divine love is illicit, passionate love. Such love strikes like lightning, blinding one to the duties of married life and carrying one away even against one's will. This quality of love was celebrated by the poet Jayadeva, who sang of the young God incarnate Krishna enchanting all the young wives in the region with his amorous glances and flute playing. At night, hearing seductive melodies from his flute, they would steal away from their husbands' beds and, in a moonlit glade, dance and make love with their celestially resplendent, dark young God. Here, instead of burning in Hell the unfaithful wives are assured of Heaven.

This attitude of divine passion spread to the Muslim world, where it was celebrated by the Sufis under the name *fanā*, or the passing away of the self, and it became the theme of mystical Arab love poetry and song. In these verses the lover burns for his absent beloved; and the farther the distance, the more his love increases. One of the main centers where this impassioned lyricism blossomed was Andalusia in tenth- and eleventh-century Moorish Spain. From Spain this passionate attitude and its poetry had only to cross the Pyrenees to arrive in the feudal courts of southern France, stir the hearts of dutifully married ladies and their admirers, and encourage them to celebrate and sing of their illicit love. So it was that in the courts of Provence in southern France the cult of courtly love bloomed toward the end of the twelfth century.

A Western reader, steeped in the doctrines of romantic love through movies, popular music, literature, and most of all by the way people behave, will have difficulty seeing anything novel about courtly love. After all, isn't it natural that a young man should praise his beloved in song, and that love should be a central literary theme? A reader from a tribal society, from traditional China or Japan, or from the milieu of Plato, Aristotle, or St. Paul would simply not ask that question. For what began quite suddenly at the end of the eleventh century in Provence was something unique in the history of human sentiment and literature. The Western deference to women shown in opening doors and other acts of courtesy that springs from Provençal *cortezia* is nowhere to be found in other societies. The Indian husband may be told to treat his wife like a Goddess, but she does not sit at the same table "with him." Before the advent of courtly love the enduring themes of Western literature and song were fraternal, Platonic, and divine love. Love between a man and a woman rarely rose above the level of carnal hedonism in ancient literature, in which women were not objects of devotion but of voluptuous merriment—good perhaps for a roll in the hay but forgotten the moment a man was called to battle or prayer. And while the value of a steadfast wife was sometimes admitted, as in *The Odyssey*, the homecoming of Odysseus to Penelope was subordinate to the manly ordeals faced by a fraternity of brave warriors returning home from war. When passionate love did occur, the ancients tended to look upon it as a sickness akin to insanity.

In India passionate love was directed toward the divine, resulting in unitive rapture. But the Western cult of *amor* was not directed toward some God. Nor was it the Christian duty to love one's neighbor (and any neighbor will do). Nor was it the equally unselective, lustful animal urgency. Rather it involved the expression of personal love for a particular and unique human creature. It was a love based on individual choice rather than ecclesiastical or societal authority and dared to stand up against those dictates. Medieval lovers simply ignored the mythology of the Virgin and her Hell which had been forced upon them. Instead, they returned to their native, pre-Christian mythology of seeing divinity within nature and innocent human love.

The tragic story of two medieval lovers, Héloïse and Abelard, illustrates the conflict between the two opposing mythologies. Abelard, in his late thirties, was a gifted Parisian intellectual. He seduced Héloïse, a beautiful woman of eighteen. She became pregnant and he advised that they should marry. She refused, saying that she would rather be his mistress than cause him, a philosopher, to stoop to matrimony. In the meanwhile Héloïse's uncle had Abelard castrated. Then Abelard sent Héloïse to live in a convent. Not hearing from him for years, Héloïse broke the silence with a letter stating that she did not love God but him, and that she would endure the flames of Hell if only she could be with him. She was willing to defy all authority. Only Abelard, who had been motivated by lust, clung to the old mythology and bowed to the social conventions of his time.

In Héloïse's attitude of reliance on her own choice in love, even if in opposition to the sacred authority of the Roman Catholic Church and the sacrament of marriage, we find the first ray of light of the Renaissance. *Amor*, after all, is the reverse spelling of Roma.

The cult of *amor* did not remain confined to the courts of southern France. It blossomed throughout a medieval Europe in which Christian credo had been forcibly imposed by Constantine and the Carolingian emperors on entire populations still stirred by pagan passions. And we are still eating the fruit of that flowering of love between knights in shining armor and fair damsels blowing kisses from the ramparts of castle towers. For *amor* or *cortezia* slowly became transformed into the uniquely Western set of values known as romantic love. Although men no longer ride about in shining armor dedicating all their knightly deeds to some fair maiden in a tower, the entire web of modern literature, entertainment, etiquette, song, and sentimentality is woven from the gleaming strands of courtly sentiment and binds us to an eternal quest for a happiness based on successful romantic love. Our pursuit of love is so tacitly impelled by this myth that we never question it. We never guess that our most ardent dreams, deepest aspirations, and most meaningful actions are but dramatizations of its silent and insistent demands. So charmed are we that we will gladly forget Platonic love, divine love, brotherly love, sisterly love, paternal love, conjugal love, familial love, self-love, and even sexual love in order to fulfill our most sacred quest. We never see beyond the veil of this force that enchants and possesses us. For one of its demands is that we want only to succumb more fully, to be more completely disarmed, and more deeply hypnotized. Yet to inquire, to see the naked truth of the myth, to expose the conflicts and anxieties that we as its dramatis personae subject ourselves to is to begin to evaporate the spell, to free the heart from its bewitching illusions, and to find that the myth, like a mirage, promises a reality it can never present.

Whence, then, this fascination with an idealized eroticism that promises to transfigure us and make us live more fully and intensely? From what elements are its most binding threads woven? Courtly love was first popularized in songs by troubadours in praise of their highly idealized and unattainable women. The troubadour would sing of his devotion to a woman, praise her goodness and beauty, pledge complete enslavement, lament her disdain, vow to become ever more virtuous for her sake, and dedicate to her his knightly deeds. Such love was a mockery of the values of Christian marriage and monastic asceticism. While Christian monastic love was dependent on a depersonalized yearning for a transcendent power, and marriage was more often than not a loveless duty, courtly love promised a devotional passion that was more earthly and intimate than Christian devotion, for it was directed to a living human being. While the Church was telling the compulsorily converted that passionate love even for one's own wife is an unspeakable sin, the troubadours said that true passion is totally opposed to marriage, for it can result only from adultery. And whereas the Church condemned every sexual act that was not solely for the purpose of procreation, the troubadours sang of the purifying powers of passionate human love. Thus the cult of *amor* was nothing less than a religious passion. The young knight or troubadour must set his lady above all else. Moreover, the knight or troubadour must be chaste with respect to his lady, though he may have engaged many a peasant woman in a roll in the hay. The relationship between the lover and his beloved had to be chaste because the loved one was always unattainable—usually a lady already married to the lord of a castle. Courtly love, then, was based on a form of chaste adultery and inflamed by a passion that ignored society, morality, and even happiness. The long tradition of passionate, unhappy, and often fatal adultery as *the* theme of Continental literature stems from courtly love.

Another reason chastity was observed in courtly

love is that the lovers were really not concerned with the carnal satisfaction of passion, for that would put an end to it. Rather than satisfaction, these lovers desired the prolongation and emotional intensification of passion. If this passion was consummated, the beloved would cease being an object of transcendent adoration and descend to the status of a mere woman. As one poet of the period put it, "He knows truly nothing who wants to possess his lady. Whatever turns into reality is no longer love." Thus courtly love most resembles that of adolescents during the 1950's when it was yet chaste and brimming with fear of and yearning for unknown pleasures. Both types of love are inflamed by obstacles—by whatever thwarts satisfaction—thus making passion all the more consuming.

Distance is the obstacle par excellence. The courtly lover waits patiently and loves with chaste devotion. He waits for someone who is not and will never be available—the faraway princess, the maiden in the tower, or, in her more modern incarnation, the blonde flashing by in the red Ferrari observed by the man who is walking down the boulevard hand in hand with his fiancée. Since these lovers seek not their beloved's presence but their absence, we must ask a rather odd question: Do they love one another?

Denis de Rougemont, in *Love in the Western World,* has argued cogently that truly they do love, but not one another. What they love is the awareness of loving—the *state* of being in love—more than the beloved, who is valuable and precious only as long as she serves as an instrument for the lover's own self-exaltation. While these lovers are seemingly obsessed with each other, their passion only masks a dual narcissism. It promises a happiness that it can deliver only in a mystical dimension.

One of the earliest troubadours sang, "Of love I know that it gives great joy to him who observes its laws." Chastity was one of those laws, yet it was a type of chastity in which a ritualized love was practiced by at least some. A troubadour would gaze long and lovingly at his beloved; deep emotion would well up between them. He would then undress her and press her naked body close to his. They would lie together for hours in a chaste embrace. In this way the troubadour possessed the vital joy of his beloved without intercourse. The purpose of such love is expressed by William of Poitiers, an early troubadour: "I want to retain my Lady in order to refresh my heart and renew my body so well that I cannot age. He will live a hundred years who succeeds in possessing the joy of his love." This technique is similar to certain mysticoerotic techniques practiced in China and India to achieve health, longevity, and spirituality. We will explore these in the chapters that follow. As already mentioned, there may well have been an historical connection between the troubadours' religion of love and the sexual wisdom of the East. Courtly love also resembles the early Christian practice of men taking to themselves *agapetae*, or virgins, and enjoying with them *coitus reservatus*, a contemplative embrace avoiding genital orgasm. The Church repressed this practice only to see it resurface in the cult of courtly love.

In modern romantic love, joy is equated not with chastity but with passion, sensuality, and orgasm. Thus much European and American literature, stage, screen, and song is but a vulgarization and popularization of courtly love. No longer do readers of modern novels and viewers of movies value Chastity, Moderation, and Patience. We demand a plot full of suspense, sensuality, and a happy ending. Yet passion is still the supreme quest that every real man and woman must attain if they are truly to live. Bombarded as we are with the propaganda of romantic love, we seek the challenge of the unattainable and forbidden, forgetting all about divine, Platonic, fraternal, conjugal, and self-love. Can we imagine Vladimir Nabokov's Lolita as an available woman of marriageable age? Can we visualize Romeo and Juliet without the numerous obstacles they faced, and their eventual death?

At the same time that we are bombarded with the myth of romantic love, we are blasted with what is called middle-class morals, extolling the virtues of marriage, of growing accustomed to his or her face, a face once so mysterious, fugitive, and vulnerable. But the two systems, romantic love and marriage, are irreconcilable. The unattainable passion, once attained, becomes the merely familiar. We have only to recall our age-old desire to travel to the distant moon, to find upon our arrival there, nothing so lovely and compelling as the full earth rising, far, far away.

Thus we are impelled by two conflicting moralities: the ethics of marriage, commanding eternal fidelity, and the impinging ethics of passion, requiring a rabid enchantment with an ever-elusive quarry.

Romantic love denies reality, depending on an overevaluated image of the beloved. Romantic love, we are told, does not change; it is eternal. Yet, in reality, it does change. It often flees just as the first signs of age stealthily appear on the countenance and limbs of the beloved, depriving him or her of youthful beauty. Romantic love, we are told also, is the very essence of joy, but often it brings sadness, anguish, loss of independence, even death—especially when it must face reality. Frequent sexual relations with one's beloved are supposed to make romantic love grow, but often they make love diminish through familiarity. Romantic love demands dedication, eternality, unbridled passion, and the deification and adoration of the beloved, especially his or her physical beauty. Romantic love is concerned with intense, passionate feelings; marriage must deal with in-laws, cleaning the bathroom, changing diapers, shopping, finances, laundry, and the reality of another person. The romantic lover sees the beloved only when he or she is well rested and well dressed. Marriage is based on domesticity and requires seeing one's spouse in unflattering moments.

Few are able to live up to the perfectionistic ideals of the romantic myth and many who do not suffer feelings of guilt, failure, and inadequacy. Some simply will not marry because they cannot fulfill their romantic ideals in the framework of marriage. If already married, they may resent their vows. Still others, whether married or single, will nourish a feeling of intense love for someone they will never be close to in reality. And yet all our popular entertainment and sentimental literature insist that a marriage based on romantic love is the goal of life. When we realize that a great percentage of psychiatric patients suffer from the conflicts that result from attempting to reconcile these two value systems, we would be wise to examine their influence in our own lives.

We have seen that marriage requires stability, familiarity, and loyalty, whereas romantic love feeds upon "obstacles." The greatest obstacle thwarting the satisfaction of passion in courtly love was Chastity. This "obstacle" was self-imposed to make the woman eternally unattainable and thus forever desirable. Modern romance, lacking this hindrance, seeks the unattainable in multiple conquests. Yet for the Don

Juan, each successive conquest is too painlessly and carelessly accomplished. The heat of his desire is never sufficiently sustained, and exhausts itself before it has consumed even the kindling. It never gets the chance to become inflamed a millionfold, feeding on the contemplation of an eternally evasive beloved.

The propaganda of romantic love is also largely responsible for perpetuating the images of desirable sex roles. The modern young man may play the knight in shining armor. Lacking a coat of mail, he grows about himself a kind of macho emotional armor. The young woman plays the sweet, weak, and submissive princess. He plays the kind of knight that she thinks the kind of princess she is playing would esteem. And she plays the kind of princess that he thinks the kind of knight he is playing ought to adore. They play harder and harder, each admiring in the other the qualities that they must fear and repress in themselves. He can never lay claim to his carefully hidden intuitive, emotional, soft, and submissive attributes. She can never realize her secretly suppressed rational, vital, and aggressive characteristics. By perpetuating his role of knight, the male is always assured of the company of a submissive female to prop up his masculinity. By excluding her from the tough and aggressive world of daily affairs, he eliminates one-half the human race from competition in that arena. He also gains a sure supply of free domestic labor and sex. By perpetuating her role of docile princess the female is assured of being perpetually protected and repressed by her prince. The moment she begins to recognize and act upon her so-called masculine tendencies, which earlier she could only admire in him, she risks overthrowing his little kingdom. And as soon as he awakens to his own so-called feminine nature, which before he could only observe in her, he risks losing her admiration. The woman who marries what seems in her timid youth to be a pillar of strength often awakens in later life to the harsh realization that she has landed a distant, uncommunicative, and oppressive bore who will deny her the opportunity to exercise any of the "masculine" muscles she now feels bulging within herself. And so it is that the middle-aged man trudges through the door, hangs his hat on the rack, and exclaims, "Honey, you know, all these years you were right—it just isn't out there," only to have her pick up the hat and march out the door saying, "The hell it isn't!"

Perhaps it is necessary to maintain what are termed masculine and feminine traits in mutually isolated stereotypes in order to feed the fires of youthful passion, but wherever these traits have been homogenized in one psyche we often find a whole individual possessing a blend of fluidity and firmness that transcends tacitly accepted sexual roles and springs from a deep personal integrity. Many male saints, artists, and seers, for instance, have had to go beyond stereotypical masculine roles in order to touch the so-called feminine founts of their souls. It is no accident that the word for "soul" in many languages is of feminine gender—Greek *psyche,* Latin *anima,* and Spanish *alma*—for the mystical relationship between the human spirit and the deeper currents of the flow of life is one of submission and surrender. Men must learn that reclaiming the "feminine" side of the male psyche is not at the expense of but an enhancement of the power of the personality.

The Confessing Animal

Sex provides a strong fulcrum for those in positions of power. Thus the Catholic Church was not
content simply to condemn sex. It was necessary to
make people admit their sexual transgressions. Expecting women to be copies of the Virgin, yet believ-
ing them to be descendants of Eve, the Catholic
Church in the thirteenth century developed the ritual
of obligatory confession. At first, this dutiful little ceremony was simple enough. In the sexual sphere there
was not much to confess. Lustful acts were simply
considered sinful and confessional acts, purifying. In
the eternal battle between power and pleasure, it
would seem that power was finally and firmly in command. However, as we observed in the rebellion of
the cult of *amor* against the Church, repressed pleasure has a tendency to spring back with redoubled
force. Therefore, the institution of confession only
succeeded in inflaming the sexuality it sought to quell.
Michel Foucault has demonstrated in *The History of
Sexuality* that confession succeeded only in vitaliz-
ing an insatiate sexuality that reveled in defiant exposure. For the very act of confession was a verbal
exposure and an elaboration of sexuality. Sex, which
before had been a massively solid, single, uniform, and
unspeakable evil, was suddenly subjected to rigorous
self-examination and minute analysis. Before, there
had been only the sin of the sexual act; now, trans-
gressors began to confess all its subtle, possible, and
depraved nuances—positions, partners, fantasies, fe-
tishes. Whereas once there had been only the sinner,
now there was the pimp, the adulterer, the mistress,
the harlot, the homosexual, the sodomist, the . . . The

monolith of sexuality became dissected, splintered, atomized into a myriad polymorphous perversities. Not only were sexual acts sinful—but suddenly so were sexual desires and fantasies. The entire domain of sinfulness had been multiplied a thousandfold overnight.

Against the power that interrogated, pried, inquired, searched out, and examined, there arose the pleasure of defiantly evading, quibbling, and violating. One of the most delectable forms of violating the campaign against sex was to use the ritual of the confessional to show off one's chosen perversity, denude it, and wag it before the inquisitor. Western society thus developed a fondness for confession. It satisfied the inquisitor's lust for power and the confessor's need for defiance and purgation. And not only did Westerners confess in church, but with the Protestant Reformation, confession was no longer ritualized and localized in the confessional. We began to confess before judges, doctors, teachers, parents, and lovers. Western society became the confessing society, bearing its sins, crimes, pains, pleasures, troubles, and transgressions. And almost every sphere of Western life—family, education, religion, medicine, literature, psychology, and philosophy—extracted such confessions, multiplying the realm of sexuality a millionfold. The discourse of the pervert was not only registered in the confessional, but became subjected to judicial inquiry, clinical examination, psychological analysis, theoretical elaboration, and literary popularization. Can we think of *Lolita* without its confessional character?

The Church preached that any sexual act that was not within marriage and for the cause of reproduction was fraudulent and perverse. However, as a result of the growth of sexuality, each perversity became observed, classified, and finally institutionalized. Each category of perversity emerged from obscurity and became a species in its own right, with a label, a corpus of research, and a right to self-determination.

As each new aspect of sexuality was brought to light and published, not only did it then assume a life of its own, but the institutions that observed, classified, and discussed it reaffirmed their power—and this was especially true of the medical profession. After all, if members of Western society wish to learn everything they want to know about sex but are afraid to ask, they need only consult any number of informative books on the subject, more often than not written by male medical doctors. Leafing through the pages, they will find what has been confessed over the centuries to members of the medical profession. It seems that the truth of sex is finally available in the form of a science of sex, complete with anatomical illustrations and Latin names. Yet the more discourse there is concerning sexual matters, the more important sex becomes and the more there appears to be a secret that eludes us. We have an insatiable thirst to understand and enjoy sex, thinking that through it we will transcend all power and authority. We never guess that the sexual knowledge and conventions we consciously and unconsciously incorporate may be subjecting us to conformity and conflict.

The morality of marriage, the myth of romantic love, and our ever-increasing knowledge of sex have fused to generate an image of marriage as a sort of congenial genito-romantic paradise. The magic formula to enter this realm reads something like: happiness = sex; sex = thrusting intercourse and orgasm. This formula is repeated again and again, and so becomes the most secret incantation of our hearts. Let us examine the terms of this formula in order to determine its truth.

Happiness = Sex

The field of psychotherapy has been largely responsible for putting an overemphasis on sex as the key to personal happiness, encouraging patients to find the source of their conflicts in sex while neglecting other problems. It is little wonder people conclude that unhappiness is always the result of some variety of sexual dysfunction. The person seeking professional guidance may be advised to use conventional sex to release tension that may actually have its origin in a totally separate domain. Yet if the cause of the problem is continually ignored, he or she may begin to feel that there is some exotic form of sexuality that must be experienced in order to produce true happiness.

We are expected to find personal fulfillment through sex. Yet many people do not feel as sexual as they are told they should feel, especially the type of person psychologist Dr. Abraham Maslow calls "self-actualized." These are individuals who have developed their full potential. Because they are more fulfilled and creative in many other areas of life, sex tends not to be a pressing need. Yet for the self-actualizing person, orgasm is both more and less important than for most people. It is more important because it is experienced more fully, as a deep mystical feeling or what may be called a "peak experience." But for the self-actualizing person, sex is but one avenue to the peak experience. Thus sex is profoundly enjoyed,

though it is not felt to be necessary for personal fulfillment. In fact, many of the world's most creative,
vital, and happy individuals have been monks and
nuns, celibate by choice.

Contrast this with the person who must hungrily
engage in more and more complex and exotic sexual
experiences, searching for a happiness that never
seems to arrive. One may read countless books on sex,
experiment with novel positions and techniques, and
change sexual partners frequently, never guessing that
happiness is something that cannot be squeezed out
of sex like so much water from a sponge. Such a seeker
of sexual happiness may thirst for newer and newer
experiences and begin to look for quantity rather than
quality. Those forms of sexuality that seem forbidden—homosexuality, adultery, and incest—may then
be considered. But in a sexually promiscuous society
in which nothing is left forbidden, the seeker of taboo pleasures will sooner or later reach the end of
the line.

And so today, when people can have as varied a
sex life as they want, many have become so bored with
sex that members of the sexual avant-garde such as
Andy Warhol and Mick Jagger have come out as celibate. Whereas during the 1960's, virginity was something of an embarrassment, in the 1970's, it was back
in vogue, and an American Virgin Liberation Front was
formed in order to help virgins maintain a healthy self-
image and establish their freedom to remain chaste.
It was found that many young women who had
undergone a period of sexual promiscuity in order to
lose the stigma of virginity soon began to yearn for
their lost innocence. After becoming disillusioned with
sex, they again became chaste, withholding further
sexual intimacy in favor of marriage or a long-term re-

lationship. And a trend toward more stable relationships has been additionally encouraged by fear of infection by diseases such as herpes and AIDS. Thus from the early days of Christian celibacy and the equally chaste medieval cult of *amor,* we have gone on to experience a sexual revolution and increasing sexual promiscuity only to return to more conservative sexual attitudes.

Does happiness, then, equal good sex, or is it that good sex is just one of the many forms of loving expression between two happy, healthy individuals? We have been led to expect much more from sex than it is capable of delivering in and of itself. Rather than being obsessed with the variety and novelty of sexual experience, we should be concerned with the quality of being and emotion we bring to it. Are we approaching sex with an empty heart in order to get something? Or are we approaching our lover in the fullness of being in order to give him or her of that fullness? It might be wiser for members of the psychiatric profession to try to free their patients from all forms of debilitating behavior, including degenerative forms of sex, rather than blame all problems on sexual aberrations. Equal attention should be paid to diet, exercise, rest, and overall life-style as well as to sexuality, for only a state of general well-being is capable of supporting a deep and satisfying sexual relationship. In this regard those giving attention to normalizing their overall life-style would do well to engage in a regenerative style of sex such as described in the final chapter of this book.

Sex = Thrusting Intercourse and Orgasm

We do not generally think of hugging, caressing, kissing, embracing, fondling, and touching as being "the real thing" or as "going all the way." This is partly because petting is not forbidden by parents during adolescent years, while intercourse often is. Coitus is to be saved for marriage. Many young women, of course, maintain technical virginity for years, although they may spend hours a day fully naked with a man and be fully orgasmic. As long as there are men around who prefer to marry such women, and as long as these demi-virgins prefer to marry men with such perferences, theirs will remain a viable strategy. No matter how many hymens it may save, however, putting off "the real thing" for so many years has at least two negative consequences. First, it causes curiosity and expectations about intercourse to grow unrealistically high. Many young women report that their experiences of intercourse are never as pleasurable as the petting they did as teenagers. Second, once intercourse does become integrated into sexual relations, other sexual activities may become abbreviated if not abandoned altogether. When a young man has achieved the taboo goal of intercourse, why bother with mere preliminaries?

Intercourse became considered "the real thing" not because it is "going all the way," but because it is the only reproductive and thus the only religiously sanctioned way to have sex. Early Christianity taught that any other form of sexual gratification is simply a fraud against God—a perversion. We must remember here, however, that theology is the work of males, and while it is true that, lacking divine intervention, intercourse is necessary for reproduction, orgasm is not—at least not female orgasm.

Since fertilization is necessary for the continuation of the species, and since not every sexual act results in fertilization, some biologists have argued that it would have been wise for nature to create a situation in which females are denied satisfaction during intercourse, thus feeling the need for as much of it as possible. Again, it would have been wise had nature designed intercourse so that it could provide the masturbatory stimulation the male requires to ejaculate as quickly as possible. In this manner the females of the species would be capable of collecting the maximum amount of semen, thus enhancing the chances of continuation of the species, since for a small, vulnerable group in a hostile environment, a high rate of reproduction is a necessity.

Female chimpanzees in heat may copulate repeatedly with every male in the tribe for ten days in succession. The males thrust for about thirty seconds, ejaculate, then go off into the bushes to recuperate. The more process-oriented females take on one such goal-oriented male after another only to become more and more aroused. Finally, the entire male population is sexually exhausted.

In humans if a woman does have an orgasm during intercourse, the contractions, which pulse downward, tend only to push the penis and semen down and out. If, on the other hand, she doesn't come to orgasm, the swollen lower portion of her vagina will act as an obstruction, disallowing the outflow of semen.

For whatever reason, many human females simply do not experience orgasm during intercourse, but are nevertheless subjected to the myth that coitus is the

only natural way to have sex. Thus our civil laws condemn noncoital sex. Because intercourse has become
judicially institutionalized as the only natural, moral,
and healthy expression of physical affection, providing guaranteed genital satisfaction for the male and
reproduction of the species, female orgasm, if it is
considered at all, is naturally expected to happen
during copulation. The female in whom it doesn't occur is often considered even by herself to be psychologically disturbed.

Another reason intercourse is thought to be the only
valid form of sexuality is because Freud argued that
vaginal orgasm is the valid sexual response of a mature, maternal, feminine, and normal woman, while
clitoral orgasm is the characteristic sexual response of
a neurotic, infantile, and frigid woman. Freud wrote,
of course, during the Victorian era, when piano legs
were prudently provided with skirts and male and female authors separated on bookshelves. During this
era women were subjected to clitoridectomies in order to prevent "feminine hysteria." According to
Freud, the locus of genital pleasure in little girls is
the clitoris. But as a girl makes the transition into mature womanhood, she should reorient sexual primacy
from the highly sensitive and nerve-packed clitoris to
the relatively nerveless vagina. This is somewhat
analogous to saying that a mature man should achieve
orgasm through stimulation of the scrotum alone. Thus
began the heated anatomo-politics of the female sexual response. Even if Freud's seminal insights were
refuted (and we shall see that they were), nevertheless they served the time-honored tradition of ensuring a means of facile male orgasm. For his claims
seeped into the cultural mythology and to this day
they have colored the image of what sex should be

like. This model thrives in the imaginations of both men and women, is talked about in locker rooms and portrayed in popular erotic literature. Harold Robbins is a master of the genre and a foremost sex "educator." He writes:

> Gently her fingers opened his union suit and he sprang out at her like an angry lion from its cage. Carefully she peeled back his foreskin, exposing his red and angry glans, and took him in both hands, one behind the other as if she were grasping a baseball bat. She stared at it in wonder. *"C'est formidable. Un vrai caon."* . . . She almost fainted looking down at him. Slowly she began to lower herself on him. His legs came up . . . as he began to enter her. . . . It was as if a giant of white-hot steel were penetrating her vitals. She began to moan as it opened her and climbed higher into her body, past her womb, past her stomach, under her heart, up into her throat. . . . She began to climax almost before he was fully inside her. Then she couldn't stop them, one coming rapidly after the other as he slammed into her with the force of the giant body press she had seen working in his factory. . . . Somehow she became confused, the man and the machine they were one and the same and the strength was something else she had never known before. And finally, when orgasm after orgasm racked her body into a searing sheet of flame and she could bear no more, she cried out to him in French,
>
> "Take your pleasure with me! . . . Quick, before I die!"
>
> A roar came from deep inside his throat and his hands tightened on her breasts. . . . Then all

his weight seemed to fall on her, crushing the breath from her body, and she felt the hot on-rushing gusher of his semen turning her insides into viscous, flowing lava. She discovered herself climaxing again."[1]

Men and women learn from such literature 1) that women like it hard, violent, and fast; 2) that genuine sexual sharing experiences no ebb and flow of excitement but builds unremittingly in intensity, leading to simultaneous orgasm; 3) that sex should have no moments of tenderness and caring; and 4) that, as Tolstoy once remarked, "Many people's love would be instantly annihilated if they could not speak of it in French." Yet this thrusting model of intercourse, while just the grist for the mill of male ejaculation, is less ideally suited for the full range of eroticism. When one considers that only 1.5 percent of all the women interviewed in *The Hite Report* masturbated by vaginal insertion alone, and that only 30 percent could experience orgasm regularly from intercourse—it is not difficult to see what gender the thrusting model of intercourse serves. Sex, as prescribed for men and women in much of the sexual propaganda of popular culture, is simply sex for males—concerned with the prompt production of ejaculation. In the unvarying sequence of 1) foreplay, 2) penetration, and 3) intercourse, foreplay often is only used to produce sufficient lubrication for penetration and, thus, a pleasurably moist mass of female protoplasm with which to masturbate. The word "foreplay" itself is a term that helps institutionalize this model, for it implies that anything short of thrusting intercourse and orgasm is not "the real thing," and is not pleasurable in and of itself. Unless a woman can experience orgasm during intercourse, there is no place for her to do so in this peni-centric model of the sexual universe.

Freud's insistence that there are two kinds of female orgasm, clitoral and vaginal, was rejected by the findings of Dr. William H. Masters and Mrs. Virginia E. Johnson in *Human Sexual Response.* In their view the distinction between clitoral and vaginal orgasm is false. In fact, the researchers found that anatomically all female orgasms are centered in the clitoris. Thus any orgasms that take place during intercourse are produced by indirect clitoral stimulation, not vaginal stimulation. They also provided clinical proof that many women are multiorgasmic and that the intensity of orgasm is greatest during masturbation, followed by manual stimulation by a partner, and least of all by sexual intercourse. Freud's theories seemed to have been refuted overnight.

Feminists were happy with these findings because in theory they freed woman's sexuality from dependence upon vaginal stimulation and thus from the necessity of a man's erect penis. Woman's sexual pleasure, at least orgasmic pleasure, was now independent of man's, and women had the right and responsibility to seek their own gratification as ardently and aggressively as every man sought his. Yet this new knowledge could not be embodied by the general population—this new sexuality could not become actual sex—without new generally accepted models of both sexual intimacy and intercourse. Males had to relinquish their peni-centric conditioning and find genuine enjoyment in exploring more subtle nuances of physical intimacy. Females also had to free themselves from blind or unwilling acceptance of the male pattern of sex and take responsibility for their own enjoyment. They had to resist deferring to whatever model of feminine sexuality men offered them, and learn that there is nothing particularly mysterious about female orgasm. It simply requires the right kind of stimulation, which is most often not provided by thrusting.

The era of clitoral primacy was ushered in. Many women began demanding adequate clitoral stimulation and expecting that they should experience orgasm in every sexual encounter. Many men became adept at providing such stimulation, and also expected their partners to have an orgasm each time. In fact, couples began chasing after orgasm. Many abandoned the typical in-and-out, battering-ram method of thrusting, and engaged in intercourse in which the two bodies press together (penis inside the woman) in such a way that the clitoris receives continuous stimulation through the pressing together, rubbing, and grinding of both pubic areas. The couples began enjoying prolonged and deep penetration without thrusting, but with rhythmic, soft, and increasingly firm pressure. This approach, compared with thrusting, provides little stimulation to the penis and thus allows the male to delay orgasm indefinitely. Since the "era of the clitoris," couples have also enjoyed many forms of noncoital sex, such as manual and oral stimulation. Then, just as women thought the myth of the vaginal orgasm had gone the way of the dinosaurs, along came the popularity of the Graftenberg spot, or G spot, a sensitive area in the vagina midway between the cervix and the top of the pubic bone. The debate concerning vaginal-versus-clitoral responsivity was rekindled.

When a woman is unaroused, the G spot is about the size of a dime or quarter. When she becomes sexually excited, however, this spot increases in area, and stimulating it can give intense pleasure leading to orgasm. Many women find that the G spot is too sensitive to be stimulated prior to clitoral orgasm. Once clitoral orgasm takes place, however, such arousal is highly satisfying. However, intercourse that stimulates this highly responsive area might actually cause discomfort, if clitoral orgasm has not occurred.

The missionary position is probably the worst for arousing the G spot, for the penis must stimulate the front wall of the vagina. Better are rear-entry positions and those in which the woman sits astride her lover. The best position requires a surface, such as a table, that is hip high to the male. The woman lies on her back and drapes her legs over her lover's shoulders as he stands and follows her indications of how deep and at what pace to proceed. This position also grants easy access to the clitoris, which can be touched by either partner.

With the popularity of the G spot, the age of clitoral primacy was over and the era of the vaginal orgasm began. Many couples began producing chains of orgasms just like all the new sex literature told them they should. But in doing so, they were only subscribing to a goal-oriented sexuality concerned with the production of orgasm, especially female orgasm. A man could now measure his masculinity if his partner answered "Yes" to his insistent "Did you come?" This was not an innocent and pleasurable exploration of each other's being, but just another mechanical and athletic means to validate masculinity.

In an era following ignorance and repression of sexuality, we became a little overconcerned with orgasm. Any woman (or man) who has ever faked an orgasm will know the truth of that statement. In our enchantment with sexuality, intercourse, and orgasm, we have become concerned almost exclusively with local, genital gratification at the expense of more general, varied forms of physical affection. Through orgasm, however, we expend a tremendous amount of energy, funneling it through a very narrow, culturally defined channel. While other cultures have discovered different uses for sexual vitality, we pursue orgasms with all the fanatical zeal of athletes training for an Olympic event. The subtleties of simple and more relaxed forms of touching, hugging, and physical expressions of warmth escape us. As Germaine Greer pointed out, after all the porno flicks have been watched, all the vibrators and sexual techniques applied, all the wives swapped, sex has not changed that much. It still boils down to ejaculating seminal fluid into a vagina—like squirting jelly into a doughnut. Although many women say that emotional closeness is more important than intercourse or orgasm, they find themselves having to submit to the entire ritual of foreplay, penetration, intercourse, and orgasm—the whole doughnut ritual—in order to enjoy any kind of physical intimacy from a man. It is little wonder that for many women the model of good sex has become lesbian sex.

There is no reason, however, why nondemanding and non-goal-oriented physical intimacy cannot be enjoyed for its own sake. There is no reason why sharing physical and emotional warmth should necessarily lead to the missionary position, focused genital stimulation, intercourse, and orgasm. And there is no reason why physical pleasure should conform to a culturally ordained gymnastic performance with its rules and goals.

In submitting to the demand to perform, to provide and respond to the focused genital drive to orgasm, we overlook more subtle, diffuse, relaxed, and receptive modes of intimacy. Women seem to be more aware of this than men, and I quote here from what female respondents to *The Hite Report* have said. One woman explains that

> Good sex, for me, is much more than genital. It involves two whole bodies and two whole souls, exploring each other, sensitizing and being sensitive to each other, holding, caring for, being gentle with each other, being very aware of each other and working into a oneness that is neither and both persons.[2]

This response seems to be a total denial of the doughnut ritual. Instead, it values exploration, sensitivity, care, awareness, communication, and an almost mystical sense of oneness between "two whole bodies and two whole souls," rather than between two sets of genitals. Again, it would be a very apt description of much lesbian sex, in which foreplay is all, contraceptives are unnecessary, and fear of pregnancy is absent.

Three more responses typify the general desire among women for more whole-body contact. The first respondent reports that "long, gentle passionate encounters, with much touching and enthusiasm, give me a feeling of being loved all over and are all I need most of the time."[3] Another submits that "a really good hug I will take over an orgasm any day."[4] The third testifies that "with my present lover we spend anywhere from two to six hours caressing, touching, cuddling, and hugging, kissing, and just resting against one another."[5]

Finally, one respondent gives a clue why more

general physical closeness can be more meaningful for many women than genital stimulation.

> Closeness with another person is more important to me than orgasm (which I can have by myself if necessary). If I had to *choose* between the two, I'd choose touching. I really dig kissing, hugging, fondling, looking at, and feeling the other person. I feel like I'm sharing more if we don't get into genital stimulation, especially when first getting to know each other, because sexual arousal and orgasm takes a sort of concentration on myself so I feel more alone when I'm into that.[6]

Genital arousal and orgasm make this respondent "feel more alone." If it is true that focused genital stimulation and orgasm are separative and nonrelational compared with more communicative forms of physical intimacy, then emphasis on the former can sometimes serve to avoid deep interpersonal communion. Sexual partners who are obsessed with genital stimulation and orgasm are often caught up in a psychological disposition of separateness and use one another to achieve a nonrelational, independent, self-possessed, self-oriented "satisfaction." Obviously such satisfaction can be only partial—only a temporary release or easing of the feeling of separateness. Thus orgasm can be separative if it obliterates and replaces the unifying and relational power of desire with a blinding moment of narcissistic personal pleasure and with minimum intimacy. For the emotionally armed person, and it is usually the male who falls into this category, the entire arena of sex can be utilized to act out and momentarily transcend feelings of alienation.

A more general transmission of affection and energy by the body requires a more expansive and intimate relational capacity, and is simply blocked off. However, if the feeling and attention that are caught up in the inward disposition toward separateness could be yielded and directed instead into a relationship with someone one regards as one's intimate friend, then the obsessive need for orgasmic release, for the momentary oblivion of the sense of isolation could be annulled.

Then sex would not be based on the urge toward orgasm but on ecstatic, pleasurable, body-to-body and soul-to-soul conductivity and communion. It is unfortunate that many culturally defined sex roles and even sex manuals seem to be in a conspiracy against such sexuality. Many men, for instance, experience sex as the most important and defining test of their masculinity. They simply cannot think of physical intimacy without intercourse and orgasm. Yet these same men feel pressured to perform in this role. Such pressure disqualifies the possibility of surrender to a mutual relaxation, nondemanding exploration, and emotional sharing.

Another reason we repress whole-body pleasurableness is because of antisexual taboos we learn in childhood. We are taught that our bodies are bad, and that touching is dirty. This causes bodily tension and doubt, and we seek release during orgasm.

What is needed, then, is an entirely new and relational model of sexuality that can free people from their cultural conditioning concerning sex and allow intimate sexual partners to initiate each other into increasingly deep areas of communion. In search of this model the chapters that follow will explore sexual practices in ancient China and India, which will allow us to see our own Western conditioning more clearly. In some tribal and traditional cultures, sex is based more on the merging of bioelectric, emotional, and spiritual fields than on physical stimulation and orgasmic discharge. Finally, how can we avoid the sexual follies of other cultures while learning from their sexual wisdom ways to enrich our own rapidly evolving sexual awareness?

Clouds and Rain

*I*N ANCIENT CHINA a branch of plum blossoms is silhouetted against a full moon. Reflected in the dark lake the galaxy spews light like a dizzy cloud of fireflies. Far in the distance, horses and carriages pass almost silently. Amid the whispering fragrance of pines, a pleasure pavilion gathers the moonlight like white jade. The night deepens. A light mist rises off the lake and mixes with the pine fragrance. Now and again mountain birds cry plaintively. Soft moans arise occasionally from the pavilion. A gentle breeze penetrates the curtains and drifts through the room past a pair of golden swallows fluttering eternally on a painted screen. Behind the screen a young woman's body tenses. The golden pin falls from her hair, her eyes disappear under their lids, her nostrils widen, and her face flushes. Her lover's "jade stalk" drifts dreamily, advancing and retreating within her "solitary valley," like a fish weaving upstream against the current. The Yellow Emperor is "blending the yin and the yang" with one of his twelve hundred concubines. She opens her lips and her teeth shine. Her tongue stiffens and swells. A warm scent rises from the pillows. Her "yin tide" is flooding.

In ancient China the names of sexual organs, positions, and movements are neither coarse tabooed slang nor polite Latin terms, but images borrowed from nature that reflect the unique quality of the erotic element they symbolize. Thus it is written that "the wandering bee penetrates the floral heart," or that "the small boat weaves through the waves." These images illustrate that sexual play between man and woman is as innocent as nature.

However natural, there is a skill to this dallying. For it is said that the Yellow Emperor never ejaculated, never slept, and had the vigor of ten young men. By means of the energy derived from the art of the bedchamber, he attained an immortal body and ascended to Heaven in broad daylight. In Heaven he continued his amorous ways, this time with celestial damsels. Yet he would have been entirely ignorant of this Heaven-conferring art had not his consort, of unimaginable beauty and unfathomable wisdom, initiated him into its secrets.

To understand this ancient art of the bedchamber we must know something of the Chinese view of nature. There is, perhaps, no better way to do this than through studying landscape painting, which has been regarded as the crowning achievement of Chinese art. When the capital of China moved from Chin in the north to Nanking in the south, Taoism permeated every stratum of society and exerted a deep influence on landscape painting, or "mountain and water" painting, as it is called in Chinese. When the northern Chinese viewed the dramatic mountain peaks, the surging rivers, and the serene lakes of southern China, they responded by painting some of the most luminous and expansive landscapes ever created.

In these paintings, jagged mountains and roiling

rivers loom into view, emerging from the pearly light of clouds or floating atop celestial oceans of mist into which they seem to disappear and then reappear like ephemeral islets. Withered pines hang inverted from sheer cliffs. The viewer is left with the impression that mountain and cloud, form and emptiness, are only eternally interweaving currents of energy. The most adamant mountain erodes according to its geological nature as surely as any cloud does according to its meteorological laws. The Chinese saw in this natant dreamworld of interweaving energy patterns an ocean surging with tidal forces. This ocean of the universe is composed of *ch'i,* "breath" or "energy." *Ch'i* constantly solidifies or dissolves, warms or cools, rises or falls, ebbs or flows between two poles of energy. One pole—feminine, abysmal, passive, shadowy, moist, and symbolized by cloud, mist, valley, winter, and midnight—is called yin. The other pole—masculine, vigorous, active, sunlit, dry, and symbolized by mountain peak, constellation, summer and noon—is called yang. Everything is always yin-ing or yang-ing. With the fierce, yang heat of noon, a turning point is reached and then the yin begins to grow in proportion to yang until it reaches its maximum, and another turning point, at midnight. Movement and stillness, hardness and softness—all pairs—alternate between yin and yang.

Underlying all these yin-ing and yang-ing currents is an inactive, eternal field of spiritual energy called the Tao. It is from this empty, silent, fathomless, soft, deeply hidden, evasive, invisible, inaudible, shadowy, and obscure field that the entire universe of forms arises. Tao is the humble mother and gentle harmonizer of all things. Just as the dark vacuity of space spawns the serene and luminous galaxies, the emptiness of the womb generates a breathing child, and the teacup becomes useful precisely where it isn't—the entire universe is woven out of this deeply hidden, empty fullness.

Lao Tzu, the foremost Taoist philosopher-poet, said that nothing is softer than the Tao; it is like water. Nothing is more gentle; yet in its fluidity, nothing else has the ability to conquer the hard and strong. Living things, after all, are soft and supple; rigidity comes only near death. It is obvious from Lao Tzu's description that the Tao has many so-called feminine or maternal qualities, and he dreamed of returning to a matriarchal form of civilization that would embody these. His *Tao Te Ching* is one of a very few—and, without doubt, the earliest—books thoroughly to advocate the superiority of the feminine, the gentle, the tender, the supple, and the humble. Great strength, Lao Tzu said, only *appears* to be weak. All of Chinese culture, from painting to guerrilla warfare to sexual practice, is based on this appreciation of the feminine. For all that is yin and feminine is closer to the Tao, and superior to the seeming strength of masculinity. The feminine is softer and participates in a more subtle, pervasive, and powerful field of energy.

During the early matriarchial and aptly named yin period of Chinese history, woman was credited with having special magical power. Not only was she the nourisher of her children but, like the earth-womb, she was believed to be charged with vast amounts of vital energy. For this reason Chinese sages often retired to caves in order to meditate, and believed that animals living underground, such as foxes, tortoises, and bears, accumulate large quantities of vital energy, or *ch'i*. Because women have a lot of *ch'i*, they were also considered to be strong in *te*, or virtue, and were thus able to enchant men envious of their mysterious energy. The ancient Chinese male appraised a woman somewhat the way a modern male might assess stereo components—it is not the knobs that are important but the circuitry, not the physical features so much as the more subtle power of vitality.

An ancient book of Chinese oracles, the *I Ching* or *The Book of Changes*, uses a series of sixty-four hexagrams to depict all the possible changes of yin and yang in the universe. The hexagram representing the energy pattern of sexual intercourse between man and woman is sixty-third in the series, and is labeled Completion.

The upper three lines form the trigram *k'an*, meaning "water," "clouds," and "woman." The lower trigram, *li*, means "fire," "light," and "man." The hexagram as a whole presents a picture of perfect harmony formed by alternating yin (broken) lines and yang (solid) lines. The yin woman is atop the yang man, just as in the expression yin-yang, yin always comes first. The fire, or energy pattern of male sexuality on the bottom, will flare up with the slightest breath of wind but is easily extinguished by water. The water, or sexual energy pattern of woman, takes a long time to boil, and an equally long time to cool down. The image associated with this hexagram is that of a kettle boiling over a fire. Because the elements involved, fire and water, are antagonistic, extreme caution must be exercised—or the kettle may boil over and extinguish the fire. Therefore, the woman is on top, a position in which she may more easily pursue her own pleasure and in which the man may more easily delay his.

Another symbol of the energy pattern of sexual union is found in the expression "clouds and rain." The third century B.C. poet Sung Yu tells us the origin of this expression. It all began, it seems, when one of China's first Emperors went on an excursion to a place called Kao-t'ang. Upon arriving, he was weary from travel and fell into a deep sleep. A beautiful woman appeared in his dream, introducing herself as the fairy of Wu Mountain. She said that she had left her enchanted home to share his pillow and bed. Thereupon they fell into passionate lovemaking. When they had harmonized yin and yang, the lady departed, saying, "I live on the southern slope of Wu Mountain. At dawn I am the morning clouds, and in the evening I am the pouring rain. Each dawn and dusk I hover beneath the Yin Terrace." Then she disappeared.

In this story the clouds represent the vaginal secretions while the rain symbolizes the semen. In clouds and rain, as in the expression yin-yang, the female element precedes the male. And because rain cannot fall before clouds form, the expression symbolizes the preferred sequence of orgasm. Like clouds, the female vaginal secretions were believed to contain vast quantities of *ch'i*. Thus the many Chinese landscape paintings depicting sages wandering among high mountain peaks and breathing in the mists in order to strengthen their vitality are not much different from such poetically erotic phrases as "the dragonfly sips water," and "the butterfly sucks the peony," suggesting the male imbibing his lover's vaginal fluids.

The most ancient manuals describing Taoist sexual teachings have come down from the Han period (206 B.C.–A.D. 220), and despite puritanical Confucianist and ascetic Buddhist efforts to repress them, Taoism stubbornly persisted in Chinese bedrooms. It seems, however, that the Communists have succeeded where the Confucianists and Buddhists failed, for on her wedding night a young Communist bride will be more likely to hand her husband a book on birth control than one on the arts of the bedchamber. The sexual teachings we explore below, then, were typical of clouds and rain in Chinese antiquity, and, as the saying goes, since then much water has flown down the Yangtze.

The practices themselves are a blend of secular necessity and sacred wisdom. By the Han period, matriarchal society had disappeared and Chinese households had become polygamous. The earliest sexual teachings seem to have been concerned only with the prolongation of sexual pleasure and ensuring that the female was satisfied before the male. That way male and female emissions would intermingle and the harmony of yin and yang would be achieved. As monogamy gave way to polygamy, however, almost any man of means maintained several wives as well as a number of maidservants and concubines. If a man tried to satisfy the sexual needs of all the women in his household by conventional methods, he would soon collapse from exhaustion. On the other hand, if he failed to satisfy his women, his household would not be harmonious—and this, too, could have dire consequences. For sex in ancient China was not just regarded as an important part of life, the blending of yin and yang was the very principle upon which the entire universe and all the various fields of human existence depended for harmonious functioning. As the *I Ching* states, the sexual union of man and woman gives life to all things. The cycle of seasons, the alternation of day and night, and the ability to run a business properly or fulfill the duties of a governmental position, all depend upon the proper blending of yin and yang. If a man's household was full of fighting and bickering, he was simply not trusted. After all, if he couldn't even harmonize yin and yang in the bedroom, how could he attend to matters outside the home? We can imagine that it was a large number of disharmonious households and sexually exhausted husbands that created the need for the intervention of Taoist sagacity, because the manuals of the bedchamber address first of all the subjects of sexual exhaustion and depletion of life energy. Since women were nearly inexhaustible sources of *ch'i*, a wise polygamous husband should be able to fill himself to overflowing with energy rather than expend himself carelessly. What he needed was the right approach.

The Accumulation of Sexual Power

The Taoists taught that sexual intercourse and erotic play were powerful means of stimulating and amplifying the yin in women and the yang in men. Through orgasm, however, this accumulation of vital force is thrown off in the form of sexual fluids, which can then be absorbed by one's sexual partner. Thus if a man can absorb the yin juices of his lover's vagina while refraining from ejaculation, he wins her vital force and augments his own. As Lao Tzu wrote, alluding to the vagina as the "valley,"

The spirit of the valley never dies.
It is called the woman, the primordial female.
Her gateway is the root of heaven and earth.
Though its essence is delicate, the more one
    draws from it, the more remains.

Similarly, if a female could absorb her lover's semen,
she could augment her own vital energy. Sex was seen
as a kind of war. Evidently most females were not
much interested in accumulating spiritual energy,
since they had such a vast store of it, and since in a
polygamous household there was not much chance of
a woman's batteries being completely drained. If her
husband was skilled in the Taoist arts of the bedchamber, she could look forward to total satisfaction
whenever she desired.

But even if a woman only wanted to provide her
husband with as many orgasms and as much vital fluid
as possible—sex was still a battle. After all, a man's
sexual energy pattern is easily excited and easily extinguished by water, while woman's watery energy is
slow to come to a boil and just as slow to simmer
down. When these two energy patterns are brought
together, extreme caution is needed. If the rain (semen) falls when the clouds (vaginal secretions) are
only half laden, the female will not enjoy the sensation of orgasm. The battle for the man, then, is as much
against his relatively volatile sexual nature as against
the woman. Thus the Taoist arts of the bedchamber
advise men on how to control their own sexual nature, how to defeat their partner in the war of sex, and,
thus, how to accumulate vital energy, or *ch'i*. As mentioned earlier, *ch'i* is the basic energy of the universe, the very force of life, and it flows between yin
and yang. Being weak in *ch'i* renders one subject to

aging and disease, while cultivating, storing, and circulating *ch'i* is necessary for a happy and vital life. Practically all the ancient Chinese arts and sciences are concerned with the harmonious ebb and flow of this energy. Acupuncture and acupressure, for example, are medical attempts to align the flow of *ch'i* by stimulating certain points on the surface of the body through which it passes. The greatest sources of *ch'i* are in the atmosphere and the sexual fluids. Practicing breathing exercises and retaining the sexual fluids are important methods of accumulating *ch'i*. Therefore, ejaculation control was an important Taoist technique, for it prevented the negative effects of seminal emission, including tiredness, a buzzing in the ears, heavy eyes, a longing for sleep, a dry throat, and listless limbs. The ancient texts advise that through ejaculation a man experiences a fleeting moment of joy followed by hours of weariness. If, on the other hand, a man withholds his semen, his vitality will be strengthened, his body and mind at ease, and his vision and hearing sharpened. By quieting his passions, he will find joy in his heart. He will be able to love his women more.

How often, then, should a man ejaculate? One of the Yellow Emperor's female sexual advisors instructed him that how frequently a man emits semen depends upon his age and vitality, and the season. Men of twenty can ejaculate at maximum once every four days; men of thirty once every eight days. Men of forty can do so once every sixteen days; and men of fifty once every twenty-one days. A man of sixty should not ejaculate at all unless his vitality is still very strong. The man who can ejaculate once every three days in the spring, however, should emit only twice monthly in summer and autumn. In winter no semen should be emitted at all because at this time of year one emission will drain as much *ch'i* as a hundred emissions in the spring.

The Taoist sexual hero, then, is not the muscle-bound young playboy who, given an opportunity, recklessly spends his semen, but the vital old sage who retains his seed while still enjoying numerous erotic encounters. And this hero is often symbolized by the gnarled and twisted old pine tree that stands vi-brantly green even during the snows of winter. Hav-ing become an immortal, he rides the swirling clouds, living only on breath and dew.

Tradition has it that if a man has intercourse once without emitting the vital essence, he will accumu-late strength. If he copulates again without ejaculat-ing, his hearing and vision will improve. If thrice, all sickness will disappear. If four times, the five inter-nal organs will be at peace. If five times, the circula-tion of blood will be augmented. If six times, the waist and loins will be strengthened. If seven times, the buttocks and thighs will gain vigor. If eight times, the body will glow. If nine times, longevity will be at-tained. And if ten times, he will be able to commu-nicate with the immortal beings and Gods in Heaven. Chinese literature is replete with stories of hoary sages with snow-white hair, the complexions of young vir-gins, and the vigor of a horse, who became immortal through the arts of the bedchamber.

In pursuit of such a state, men in ancient China learned various methods of retaining semen during the sexual act. One of these methods is simply called "the deer" because a deer was considered a magical ani-mal with an abundance of *ch'i*. In Chinese art, Lao Tzu, the legendary founder of Taoism, often appears riding a deer. The vital energy of the deer was considered to be so strong that it forms extrusions atop its head in the shape of antlers. These antlers, then, are nothing but a solidification and growth of accumulated *ch'i*. The deer antlers have a counterpart in the golden halos and crowns that appear in representations of spiritual figures in both the West and East. The prominence atop the head of the Buddha again is a symbol of his vast store of spiritualized sexual energy. All these show that mundane sexual power has risen to the top of the head, even to the point of extrusion, and that the creature thus endowed has attained the sacred.

In many nomadic and hunting tribes, the medicine men and shamans wear a kind of headdress with animal horns attached; reindeer antlers and stag horns are especially common. Such a headdress is considered the most important part of the shaman's ritual dress, for a great deal of his power is contained in the antlers. Whenever a shamanic exhibition is given merely as entertainment, as it often is in the Soviet Union on official request, the shaman performs *sans* cap, thus depriving the ritual of any real ceremonial power. This is why, in ancient Chinese medicine, powdered deer antler *(Cornu Cervi)* is a potent ingredient in love potions.

Where, then, does the stag get this excess of power? One source is the position he assumes during sleep, curling his body so that the nose touches the tail, forming an unbroken circular path through which his energy flows. This circulation of *ch'i* is an important aspect of Chinese culture, including sexual yoga. What concerns us now, however, is the primary source of the deer's vitality—his habit of constantly "flicking" his tail. This movement stimulates the deer's sexual energy, sending it up the spine until it reaches the head and is transmuted into antlers. Thus the deer exercise, as practiced in Taoist circles, stimulates the sexual energy and, when performed habitually, controls ejaculation by cutting off the duct through which the semen flows. Moreover, it redirects the nerve impulse up the spine which otherwise would go into the genital contraction of orgasm. By practicing this exercise, one is "rewiring" one's nervous system in such a way that sexual conductivity is not short-circuited in the genitals, but has a chance to rise to higher regions for whole-body exchanges of energy. This does not mean that the male who practices this exercise will be incapable of experiencing orgasm, only that the need for orgasm will be less urgent.

The deer exercise can be practiced by women as well, as it stimulates the pubococcygeal (or PC) muscle surrounding the vaginal opening. An American sexologist, Dr. Arnold Kegel, reinvented the deer exercise and found that there is a positive relationship between PC muscle tone and vaginal sensitivity. He prescribed this toning exercise for women suffering from involutary expulsion of urine during coughing, sneezing, or experiencing orgasm. Not only did the PC muscle exercise solve the problem of urinary incontinence, but it also increased vaginal sensitivity and even amplified the intensity of orgasm. The PC muscle, it seems, not only stops the flow of urine in women, it also forms the orgasmic platform and contracts in rhythmic undulations during orgasm.

It is easy for a woman to locate the PC muscle by urinating with legs spread. The muscle you contract to stop the flow of urine is the PC muscle. After you have practiced stopping the flow of urine a few times, you will be familiar with what it feels like. Then you can lie comfortably on your back, insert your finger in your vagina, and contract your PC muscle. You should feel it squeezing around your finger. It may not contract very strongly, but if the deer exercise is practiced for at least six weeks, this muscle will be strengthened considerably. If you are a man, you must also locate the muscle responsible for shutting off the flow of urine. After becoming familiar with it, try contracting it when you are not urinating. You will notice that when the muscle is squeezed, the penis and scrotum are drawn up and in toward the body.

During the deer exercise, both males and females should also contract another muscle, the anal sphincter, as if trying to stop a bowel movement from coming out. This exercise should be practiced at two different tempos, slow and fast. For the slow exercise, simply sit in a chair and relax. Begin breathing in slowly and naturally through your nose. As you near the fullest point of inhalation, slowly but firmly contract the urinary and anal muscles. Hold for one or two seconds, then relax these muscles while breathing out. You may gradually build up to three seconds or more as these muscles get stronger, but never strain them or your breath. Perform a series of ten squeezes and releases at three different periods during the day.

The fast, or flutter, mode of the deer exercise is much like the slower method—except that you squeeze and release, squeeze and release, as quickly as possible. Again, this exercise should be done three different times during the day. Once you learn how to do both modes in a sitting position, you can do them in just about any position, standing or lying down, anywhere and almost anytime: while lying in bed in the morning or evening, during a traffic jam, while sitting at a desk, or even when you are talking on the telephone or playing bridge. After about six weeks you can gradually increase the number of repetitions to twenty, done three times each day.

At first, you may begin to feel a little "horny" while doing the exercises. After all, you are tensing and relaxing the same region that becomes stimulated during intercourse. After a while, however, the slight sexual arousal you may feel while performing the exercise will be replaced by a more diffuse sensation of energy ascending the spine and a warm glow spreading throughout your body. Since you are in effect rewiring your nerve impulses, the practice will prove most effective if you abstain from sex for a month or so after beginning. One important point is that you should never strain. Like any other muscle in your body, these muscles should be kept in good tone, and regular but gentle practice is mandatory. Once mastered, the exercise can be performed by the male during intercourse, though it should never be done just at the moment of orgasm. It is better to keep your breathing calm, be aware of your state of arousal, and employ the deer contractions before becoming too excited. By developing this response during intercourse, you will be redirecting your bioelectrical impulses so that you are capable of giving a woman as much vaginal stimulation as she may desire—which may be considerable if she, too, has been practicing the deer exercise to increase her vaginal sensitivity. If you practice diligently you will also provide the reproductive organs with a beneficial flow of blood, improve their health, and stimulate hormones that will give the whole body a glowing state of health. Immortality, however, is not guaranteed.

Another, less effective, technique of ejaculation control taught by the Taoists advises becoming sensitive to the point at which one is about to ejaculate and, just before reaching that point, quickly taking the two middle fingers of the left hand and firmly pressing the spot between scrotum and anus, simultaneously inhaling deeply and gnashing the teeth together strongly. The semen, though agitated, will not be emitted but supposedly return to the penis, ascend the spine, and enter the brain. The physiology of the process is discussed below.

A Taoist treatise of the T'ang period (A.D. 618–907) advises that when a man is about to ejaculate, he should close his mouth, open his eyes wide, breathe calmly, then hold his breath. Next, he should shake his hands up and down vigorously, breathe in, and press the *ping-i* acupoint one inch above his right nipple, using the index and middle fingers of his left hand. He should also gnash his teeth. Closing the mouth and opening the eyes redirects the attention and the *ch'i* to the head. Calming the breath calms the mind, thus pacifying the need to emit. Shaking the hands again redirects the *ch'i* to other parts of the body. Pressing the acupoint sends the *ch'i* into a channel other than that causing orgasmic contractions. Gnashing the teeth brings the *ch'i* to the jaw, where it is involved in contracting the strongest muscle in the body. Thus there are numerous physiological techniques that redistribute and diffuse throughout the body the *ch'i* that is concentrated in the genital region.

However, the techniques are not all physiological, and, just as in many sports, the Taoists used mental images or attitudes. Another text of the period advises that if a man considers his sexual partner to be as worthless as stone, while thinking of himself as precious as gold or jade, his semen will be less likely to move. Should it begin to do so, however, he should stop all movement. He should make love to a woman as if he were riding a galloping, runaway horse and using a frayed rein, and be as cautious as if he were standing on the brink of a deep hole full of sharp swordpoints.

Up until the middle of the Ming period, the ideal female in popular culture was sturdy, had a well-developed, even plump, figure with large breasts, a rounded belly, and ample thighs. During other periods, the ideal beautiful woman was thinner, frail, and sickly with long, slender hands, small breasts, and narrow hips. The Taoists, however, disregarded popular notions of feminine attractiveness and developed their own criteria. Since they sought to increase their vitality by augmenting their own yang *ch'i* while drawing upon the yin *ch'i* of their lovers, they sought the most yin and vital young virgins. Something of the power of a young virgin in augmenting the *ch'i* can be gleaned from the alleged manner in which jade was collected in ancient China. Jade is the most yang substance in the universe. In fact, it was believed to be the seed of the celestial dragon. The most highly prized jade was white rather than green in color. In theory, all jade belonged to the Emperor, and in the spring the imperial jade collectors would go out to find the stones. Since jade resides in veins deep below the earth's surface, rather than dig for the substance, the jade collectors would allow the powerful spring floods to do the mining for them. Then they would make a group of young virgins wade into the streams. The jade, the semen of the celestial dragon, would supposedly wash up at their feet, seeking to unite with them. If young virgins were powerful enough to draw and accumulate the seed of the celestial dragon, then just imagine how they would be able to augment the yang of a Taoist adept. Yet, if the semen was to be retained, the virgins must be handled with extreme caution. Some adepts went so far as to wear a jade ring around the base of the penis during intercourse to prevent the flow of semen.

The Taoists thought that by deflowering young virgins they themselves would take on a virginal complexion. The best partners were considered to be between fourteen and nineteen years of age. However, one should never practice clouds and rain with a woman over thirty. They also warned that one should avoid intercourse with any woman who has borne a child. The ideal bed partner is still young enough that her breasts are not yet fully formed. She should be amply fleshed, have silken hair, lustrous as lacquer, and small eyes with the pupils and whites clearly defined. Her face and body should be glowing with health, and her voice harmonious. The joints of her limbs should not protrude but be concealed in flesh. She should have either no pubic hair or such hair should be fine and smooth. Most important, she should have an abundance of vaginal fluid. She should abandon herself passionately and perspire freely during intercourse.

One should avoid women with disheveled hair, pockmarked faces, protruding Adam's apples, masculine voices, large mouths, yellow or bloodshot eyes, hair on the mouth or chin, large bones, or stiff pubic hairs. One should also avoid women given to jealousy, those with a cold pubic region, and those with ill-smelling armpits.

Since the aim of the Taoist sexual practices was to derive as much vitality from women as possible in order to gain longevity and immortality, it was considered unwise to make love with only one woman. After a while her *ch'i* would become depleted. It was better to have three, nine, eleven, or more young virgins as partners, and there were brothels that specialized in this service. The Yellow Emperor ascended to Heaven by having intercourse with twelve hundred women, and every ruler was expected to keep a large number of women in order to nourish his power. The typical emperor would have one empress, three consorts, nine wives of the second rank, twenty-seven wives of the third rank, and eighty-one concubines. Since all odd numbers are yang, or masculine, odd numbers of women further enhance the Emperor's power.

Obviously the Taoists were not interested in romantic love. For them a woman was an enemy possessing a biotherapeutic force. To have intercourse with her was to engage in battle. The only way to defeat the enemy is to keep oneself under complete control, retain one's semen, and excite her to the point of orgasm, thus gaining her yin essence.

The Taoists were lovers of peace. But at certain times during their history they were faced with the choice of being killed and their women raped—or fighting. They have always been intelligent in battle, whether sexual or military. Taoist military strategy, as used in China since the fifth century B.C., lies at the basis of modern guerrilla warfare. It was known and utilized by Mao, and is required reading for members of the Soviet military and for KGB forces. While Western businessmen look to Japanese business strategy, the Japanese read Taoist military strategy for use in their business dealings. In the West, however, it seems that men make war like they make love. It was not until 1963 that a good English translation of Sun Tzu's classic, *The Art of War*, appeared.

Taoist military strategy is very similar to sexual strategy. It is based on Lao Tzu's principle of "knowing the masculine but keeping to the feminine." Thus you must use your own force sparingly while utilizing your opponent's. Also, at first you should yield to your opponent in order to catch him or her off guard. This is the strategy one uses to swim with rather than against the current while crossing a river or negotiating a riptide in the ocean. An important Taoist treatise, the *Chuang Tzu,* tells a story that illustrates this strategy. Confucius, it seems, was viewing the beautiful scenery at Lü-liang:

> Where the water falls from a height of thirty fathoms and races and boils along for forty li, so swift that no fish or other water creature can swim in it. He [Confucius] saw a man dive into the water and, supposing that the man was in some kind of trouble and intended to end his life, he ordered his disciples to line up on the bank and pull the man out. But after the man had gone a couple of hundred paces, he came out of the water and began strolling along the base of the embankment, his hair streaming down, singing a song. Confucius ran after him and said, "At first I thought you were a ghost but now I see you're a man. May I ask if you have some special way of staying afloat in the water?"
>
> "I have no way. I began with what I was used to, grew up with my nature, and let things come to completion with fate. I go under with the swirls and come out with the eddies, following along the way the water goes and never thinking about myself. That's how I can stay afloat."[7]

This classic passage points to the difference between linear and organic movement. Linear thought

CLOUDS AND RAIN · 83

and behavior is used by the Confusianist do-gooder
who wants to impose countless rules and regulations
on life. He wants everybody to go by the book. A man
of linear thinking will measure the likely outcome of
a fight or battle by assessing the quantity of brute force
at his disposal, whether it be pounds of muscle or
megatons of explosive power.

Organic thinking and movement is more subtle. It
is like the unregimented patterns of moving water, the
forms of undulating mountains, gnarled trees, and
mists swirling together, weaving inward and outward, winnowing, turning and dissolving. It ebbs
and flows. As Lao Tzu said, "Nothing in the world is
softer or weaker than water. And yet nothing can
surpass its ability to conquer the hard and the
strong."

Organic movement is used by the judo or *aikido*
master, who may be a frail-looking octogenarian yet
capable of defeating an entire roomful of young, muscle-bound opponents by turning the force of his at-
tackers against them. An accompished master can often
throw his opponent to the floor without even touching him. The Taoists' art of fighting knows that it is
possible for a smaller force to defeat a much larger
force if the smaller force utilizes more subtle, "feminine" means. The softest and most gentle can overcome the hardest and strongest. Therefore, Taoists
emphasize stillness, withdrawal, retreat, rolling with
the punches, flowing around the object, divergence,
bending, and deflecting. Lao Tzu says that it is
better to retreat a foot than advance an inch. It may
seem that a Taoist opponent is drifting away from an
encounter, but he is actually only altering course,
turning aside in a way that will throw his enemy off-
balance so that a minimal blow will floor him.

Whereas the linear thinker will power into an enemy harbor in full daylight with all flags flying and cannons booming, the Taoist, with a much smaller force, will drift in silently with the tide in the dark of night. He will use forces already present in the environment, such as peasant unrest, to defeat the enemy, often without firing a shot. Similarly, whereas the macho non-Taoist lover will use sex and, particularly, thrusting intercourse and orgasm as proofs of masculinity; the Taoist will schedule timely pauses during intercourse to tease his opponent into a frenzy and thus win the "battle."

The story of Chang Liang, an ancient Taoist general, illustrates how Taoist principles were put into practice in an actual military situation. Chang Liang's army was surrounded by the enemy. He knew, however, that all the men in the opposing army were from the state of Ch'u, far to the south. He also knew that they had been away from home for almost ten years. What did Chang Liang do? Did he mount an all-out surprise attack with his strongest men in the front lines? No, his attack was psychological, playing upon the softest and gentlest sides of the opposing army. Chang Liang selected the very best flutists in his army, assembled them on a hill overlooking the enemy and had them play, in unison, folksongs from the state of Ch'u. Upon hearing the haunting melodies, the soldiers of the opposing army became so homesick and nostalgic that they deserted. Chang Liang viewed the opposing army in terms of its pervasive, latent emotional field. He then activated this field and watched the army break up and drift away to its native province like so much flotsam on a powerful tide. Again, the softest had overcome the hardest.

One treatise, by the Taoist Lu Tung-pin, concerns

sexual strategy to be used by the male, but it could easily be mistaken for a tract on guerrilla tactics. It states that a skilled general will not advance first but concentrate instead on drawing out his enemy, sucking and inhaling his opponent's strength. He must have an indifferent attitude, emulate a turtle withdrawing its limbs, and let his mind be as empty as the blue sky. He should be in no hurry but let his opponent throw every bit of energy into the battle and finally surrender through exhaustion. Then the succulent fruits of victory will be his to enjoy. He can withdraw from the battlefield, enriched. Only the commentary reveals that this is a sexual rather than a martial battle. "Sucking and inhaling his opponent's strength" refers to the practice of imbibing the breath and saliva of a young virgin, as these were thought to be full of *ch'i*. "Withdrawing his limbs like a turtle" refers to the practice of drawing up the genitals to lock the semen within the body. Like the skilled general, the skilled lover keeps calm while drawing out his enemy, allowing her to throw all her vital strength into the "battle" through orgasm. The "fruits of victory" are the vaginal secretions, which are imbibed by the male. "Withdrawing from battle" means that the man should then lie on his back, concentrate on absorbing the vitality won in the "battle," and diffuse it throughout his body.

Thus in the battle of love the first opponent the male must conquer is his own fiery sexual nature. We have seen that various ejaculation control techniques assisted him on this front. The other opponent he must face in battle, however, is his lover. On this front the Taoist lover utilized the principles used in the martial arts and military strategy. However, in the battle of the bedchamber the male always sought to be outnumbered by the enemy, no matter how much stronger her orgasmic force might be. For even if he were outnumbered a thousand to one, he could always win by attacking his enemy's weak spots.

Like the general who used only gentle flute music to subdue a homesick army, Taoist sexual practitioners had a thorough knowledge of the opponent, especially woman's orgasmic potential. Thus they became astute observers of female genital anatomy and sexual response, since they realized these were their opponents' weak spots. If stimulated properly, the female would gladly give herself over to passion and the battle would be won. Similarly, certain acupuncture points known as "weak spots" are used in *kung fu* and other martial arts so that the enemy can be defeated less by force than by knowledge of these vulnerable points. Blows to these areas can be fatal. Two spots, the nipples, are prime targets in both the martial and the bedroom arts, though in the latter tradition the method of attack is more subtle. In acupuncture it is forbidden to treat these points.

The uterus was called the "child door" or "child palace." The vagina was known as "the cave," the "solitary valley," or the "hidden palace." The prepuce of the clitoris was called the "dark garden," or "God field." The upper part of the vulva was the "golden ditch." The glans clitoris was the "grain," "seed," or the "mouse in the empty bowl." Knowing the anatomy of the enemy, however, was only the beginning. Such knowledge is analogous to a general's knowledge of terrain, and must be supplemented with information of the enemy's movements—the patterns of energy and stages of excitement in the battle. A master of the bedroom arts had to know the five signs, the five desires, the ten movements, and the nine essences of the female.

The first of the five signs is a flushed appearance on the woman's face. At this stage her lover may press close to her. When her nipples grow hard and her nose becomes moist, he should insert his jade stalk (penis). When her throat becomes so dry that she begins to swallow saliva, he should gently thrust. When her vagina becomes very moist, he can plunge in even more deeply. Finally, when her vaginal secretions overflow, he may draw them out.

The five symptoms of desire in a woman can also be used to monitor her response. First, if her mind desires intercourse, her breath will become irregular. If her vagina desires to make love, her mouth will open and her nostrils become dilated. If her vital energy *(ch'i)* becomes impassioned, she will move her body up and down. If her deepest heart desires to be stirred, she will emit so much vaginal secretion that her dress will become wet. Finally, when she is about to reach orgasm, her body will stretch and straighten and her eyes will close.

A skilled Taoist lover must also know the ten movements of his lover. First, she embraces the man and draws him near so that their sexual organs touch. Second, she opens her legs and indicates that she wants her clitoris stimulated. Third, she stretches her stomach. Fourth, she moves her buttocks back and forth. Fifth, she raises her legs and wants her lover to penetrate her deeply. Sixth, she squeezes her thighs together and itches inside. Seventh, she moves from left to right, indicating that she wishes the penis to strike the sides of her vagina. Eighth, she presses her torso and breasts against the man in great excitement. Ninth, she stretches her body in orgasm. Tenth, her fluids flow copiously, showing that her vital essence has been released.

The nine essences are as follows, and are important because they indicate that Taoist sexual technique was not *entirely* selfish, for it was believed that the woman's spirit was benefited as well as the man's. The first essence is indicated by deep breathing and the flowing of saliva. This is called the lung essence. The heart essence has arrived when she whispers words of endearment and sucks and kisses her lover. The spleen essence is aroused when she embraces her lover tightly with her arms. Her kidney essence is excited when her vagina becomes slippery. Her bone essence is aroused when she begins to suck on her partner's tongue. The muscle essence has arrived when she hooks her partner's body with her feet. If she begins to fondle her partner's penis, the blood essence appears. When she caresses her lover's nipples, the flesh essence is excited. When intercourse is engaged in for a long time, and the man caresses her seed (clitoris), all nine essences will have arrived. Then she will radiate all the energy of her being to her lover, and all her organs and their essences will be stimulated and harmonized. If all the nine essences do not arrive, the woman will be harmed.

In exploiting the female capacity for orgasm, Taoist males employed a number of postures, for both precoital and coital sex. These had such colorful names as "splitting the cicada," "joined mandarin ducks," and "bamboos near the altar." Some of these metaphors, such as "fluttering butterfly searching for flower," indicate that an attractive vagina was an important attribute of female beauty. The majority of these postures are ideal for stimulation of the G spot and other vaginal areas while allowing easy access to the clitoris. In light of recent Western research on the G spot, which seems to indicate that timely stimulation of this area results in copious emission of fluid, it is interesting to note that many of the postures indicated in the Chinese texts are said to cause the woman's essence to flow out like the stream called the yin tide. In fact, causing this fluid to come forth was the real goal of Taoist sexual practice, for it not only satisfied the woman but ensured the health of both partners. There is, then, an entire encyclopedia of positions for curing specific ailments within both partners. The Taoists regarded the female as a creature highly charged with *ch'i*. Since an abundance of *ch'i* keeps away diseases, the therapeutic lovemaking postures harness the immense healing energy of the woman released by her powerful sexual nature. The positions enhance this feminine energy by channeling it in various ways to stimulate specific organs or glands. The amount of energy needed to effect a cure was considerable. For instance, a typical cure for improving the circulation must be practiced nine times each day until the woman's essence appears. The woman should have nine orgasms a day for ten days. The male, of course, is not to ejaculate.

Not only are many postures indicated in the Taoist texts, but subtle nuances in rhythm and style of thrusting are described, emphasizing the Chinese awareness of constant motion and change in the universe. By varying the intensity, speed, angle, and general feel of the thrust, tedium was avoided. For instance, the man can move vigorously, like a wild horse bucking through a mountain stream. He may alternate deep and shallow strokes, like a sparrow pecking grain. He may plunge very deeply, like a huge stone sinking into the sea. Or he may veer lustily from side to side, like the long, slow swerves made by a large carp when caught on the hook. In every instance, however, these shades of motion follow fixed numerological rhythms. Since odd numbers are yang and even numbers yin, the best way to excite the female is with a series of yang thrusts. Nine shallow strokes and one deep are most commonly used. This pattern is repeated nine times during intercourse until nine times nine strokes have been completed. Other favored thrusting rhythms are three shallow and one deep, five shallow and one deep, and seven shallow and one deep. Such rhythms were highly pleasurable to the woman because of the teasing pauses during deep penetration. Counting the strokes helped keep the male's mind distracted, allowing him to retain his semen. Then his "army" of vital energy was at ease while the "enemy's" was dissipated in a thousand directions.

Readers are now aware that, for all the Taoists' adulation of the feminine principle, the sexual attitudes described thus far seem exceptionally male-oriented and selfish. One was advised not to let females know of the motivation and strategy behind these practices. Women were to have orgasms in order to provide males with as much yin fluid as possible so that they could convert this into vital energy and eventually into spirit. In fact, it was not only the vaginal fluid that was valuable. A passage known as "The Medicine of the Three Peaks" from an ancient sex manual is often quoted in early Chinese erotic prose and poetry. It views a young woman as a veritable hydraulic system, and the wise lover is instructed how to irrigate his vitality with her flows. Remember that the clouds and rivers found on mountain peaks were believed to be laden with *ch'i*. The three peaks of female anatomy not only presented a beautiful landscape, but were also reservoirs of *ch'i*. The upper peak is called

Red Lotus Peak; it is formed by a woman's lips. Its libation or medicine is called Jade Spring, and wells up from two holes beneath the tongue. When the libation flows forth, the man should swallow it to nourish his vital essence. The middle peak is called Twin Lotus Peak, the breasts. Its libation is known as White Snow or Peach Juice, and is the dew of perspiration that forms on a woman's breasts during love. (It is most beneficial to the man if his lover has not borne a child or had milk in her breasts.) Sucking this liquid benefits the male's health and vastly improves the woman's circulation. Of the three peaks, this one should receive attention first, because it will stimulate the libations of the other two. It is said that the Han minister Chuang Ts'ang lived to be 180 years of age by sucking the White Snow from a woman's breasts. The lowest peak is called Peak of the Purple Mushroom. It is also called White Tiger Grotto or Mysterious Gate, and is formed by the vulva. Its libation is called Moon Flower, and it flows from the vulva during intercourse when the woman's face becomes flushed and she murmurs in her throat. To imbibe this essence, the male should withdraw his penis so that it is only at thumb's depth. He may then absorb the libation through the skin of his penis.

In Chinese art the peach was the symbol par excellence of the vulva; it is generally larger than its counterpart of the West. The Chinese peach has a deep, opulent cleft and profuse, sweet juice. A good woman, then, was something like a good peach— plump, compliant, and above all juicy. The Taoist sage of longevity, Shou Lou, is most often depicted as a smiling old fellow. Like the deer, he transmuted his sexual energy into spiritual energy and transmitted it from his genitals to his head. Instead of sprouting antlers, however, his head has grown as large as a big melon and he is often shown holding a succulent peach, the cleft of which he fingers slyly and suggestively.

This is nothing like the romantic love we know in the West. The male was advised not to have any feelings at all for his lover, or he would certainly lose his semen and thus impede his progress toward immortality. Whereas in the West romantic love is for a specific individual in his or her uniqueness, what the Taoists required was a number of juicy young virgins. It did not really matter very much who they were. If the ancient Taoists could have heard of Western sexuality and its obsession with male orgasm, it is likely that, even though immortal, they would have died of laughter. On the positive side, the Taoist lover was sensitive to female sexual needs and was capable of satisfying all his wives, concubines, musicians, dancers, and so forth. By pleasing all his women, he benefited their health as well as his own. By having a number of wives, he did not deplete the vitality of any one. Unlike the Confucianists, who denied that females could achieve immortality, the Taoists believed women could do so by having intercourse with a number of young men while refraining from orgasm. Not many women, however, seem to have been interested in or knowledgeable about these techniques. They seem to have been content to enjoy their sexual life without seeking immortality. Their lovers believed that these practices were in accordance with the laws of nature, for if a woman submitted a measure of her abundant sexual fluids to her lover, these fluids would be transmuted into vital and spiritual energies that would radiate back to her.

The image that comes to mind here is of the process-oriented female chimpanzee who copulates with every goal-oriented male in the group until the latter are all exhausted. Chinese men seem only to have redirected their energies from seeking orgasm to the quest for immortality. While we may decry the unromantic attitude of the Taoist who considered his lover to be a mere reservoir of *ch'i,* we must remember that studies done in the West indicate that women who believe most strongly in the roses-and-candlelight approach of romantic love are far less likely to have satisfying sex lives than more realistic women. The romantic women do not talk about sex with their partners, while the realistic women communicate their needs and are active in initiating sex and seeking their own pleasure. An apologist for the Taoists could argue that they had a more realistic attitude about sex than do many Westerners, and were aware of nuances of female sexual response and details of anatomy that have only recently come to light in the West. Rather than arguing for decades over the desirability or reality of clitoral-versus-vaginal sensitivity, Taoists explored any position and method that would produce maximum pleasure in the female. Yet there seems to have been no such thing as nondemanding, nongenital sexuality. According to cosmic laws, the woman had to have an orgasm every time she had sex. Furthermore, Taoists considered her sexually obsolete at the age of thirty or whenever she had her first child— depending upon which came first. It is no wonder that the women in many polygamous households were bisexual.

What is most shocking in the Chinese treatment of women, and something that cannot be blamed on the Taoists alone, is the custom of foot-binding. This practice was common among the elite. It was a sign of status, a hallmark of a leisurely aristocratic life. The foot was bound with tape so that growth was impeded. The toes would literally rot off, and the bones of the feet would shrink in a grotesque, deformed fashion. Yet these feet were considered to be the most erotic area of female anatomy. Chinese erotic art, while depicting complete nudity and coital genital displays, never once portrays a naked female foot. Freudians explain this attitude was a form of fetishism allaying male castration fears; the bound foot is (of course) a phallic symbol. Therefore, the male reasons, unconsciously, that if his lover has a phallus (or two), then he does not have to fear having his own bitten off by the teeth his subconscious mind imagines she has in her vagina. Also, Freudians explain, the famous Heidelberg scar on a man's face is supposed to be sexually stimulating to women. They subconsciously see it as a vulva, and therefore need not fear a man's penis. Others have conjectured that the practice of footbinding was instituted to immobilize the woman, who was believed to have a practically insatiable sexual appetite. Whatever the reason for the practice, its existence should dampen any idealized notions of Chinese sagacity, for the immobility it caused could only harm the woman's health and, thus, that of her lover.

All the sexual techniques discussed above were practiced in popular, religious Taoism, but were denounced as heterodox and perverse by the more spiritually refined philosophical Taoists. The latter felt that these sexual practices constituted nothing short of sexual vampirism. During the heyday of these methods, special houses of prostitution known as "flowerboats" and "willow-houses" specialized in providing numerous young sexual partners. Also, certain Taoist sects would exchange male and female members for the purpose of spiritualized intercourse. Since the main benefit came from imbibing the sexual fluids, some Taoists went so far as to abstain from intercourse, but drink the collected sexual fluids of groups of copulating young couples. Others would drink their own semen and urine, or imbibe menstrual blood.

The typical practitioner, however, was most often a government official living in the city and surrounded by an entire harem of wives and concubines. In his heart of hearts, he dreamed of renouncing city life and becoming an immortal mountain hermit. The mountain man does not nourish himself with the yin effluvia of concubines, maids, and wives. The mere fact of dwelling among mountains provides him with ample *ch'i*. Whereas the urban Taoist imbibes the secretions of the Three Peaks, the mountain hermit nourishes his spirit by breathing in the mountain mists and clouds that rise up from the valleys every day. His sexual practice, then, partakes of the grand flow of yin and yang among the soaring peaks, and the urbanite's practice is only a poor substitute.

The typical governmental official, confined to some provincial city and harried by public and private duties, would retreat to a table in his garden, unroll the scroll of a landscape painting, like some vast pinup, and daydream that he was the sage dwelling in the bamboo hut, contemplating the undulating, jagged, mist-shrouded peaks. His garden in the city was enclosed in a courtyard and was filled with trees, clusters of rocks, hillocks, and pleasure pavilions. This was the scene of much of his erotic life. Here he could be found on a warm evening, with one of his wives leaning languidly against a tree while he approached her from behind. Other wives or maids would be present to help them in and out of various positions, and to fan them and serve them tea. They were attempting to act out as man and woman the sexual processes that were taking place within the subtle, mystical physiology of the mountain hermit.

This mystical physiology involved a process of inner alchemy, an interiorization and spiritualization of sexual energies, that finally replaced heterodox sexual techniques. The hexagram for Completion in the *I Ching* is composed of two trigrams. While the upper trigram represents water and the yin sexual nature of woman, the lower trigram stands for fire and the yang sexual proclivities of the male. The whole hexagram represents sexual union. We have seen that the same energies forming the relationship between man and woman are also found in nature, the yin moisture of the clouds, charged with *ch'i,* flowing around the soaring, phallic mountain peaks. The sexual Medicine of the Three Peaks is a replica on the human scale of the cosmic sexuality of wild mountain landscapes. The mountain hermits were able to replicate this cosmic sexuality within their own bodies. Thus the hexagram for Completion not only represents sexual union between a man and a woman, but also suggests a caldron boiling over a fire, the symbol of the process of sexual alchemy within the subtle physiology of the human body. Every transformation of yin and yang that takes place in nature and in sexual union also occurs within a single human body. Just as the earth has great flowing rivers and clouds laden with *ch'i* circulating about mountain peaks, the Chinese believed that the flow of energy, or *ch'i,* in the body follows specific channels that interweave like the tributaries of a great river system. The most obvious pathways through which the *ch'i* courses are known as meridians. There are twelve meridians, and the *ch'i* must flow unimpeded through them in constant flux if the organs associated with each meridian are to remain in good health. A blockage of the flow causes a damming up and stagnation of energy, resulting in an excess of *ch'i* in some organs and a deficiency in others. Disease is the result.

The ancient Chinese strategy for a healthy body, then, was to nourish it with adequate amounts of *ch'i* and make sure that the *ch'i* circulated rather than remained stagnant. The science of acupuncture is based on the necessity of providing an adequate flow of *ch'i.* The meridians, however, can only channel the *ch'i* to a superficial depth. The flow of energy through the twelve pathways, while necessary for maintaining physical health, is not sufficient for promoting spiritual evolution and immortality. This requires the accumulation of much vaster quantities of *ch'i* and the circulation of this energy at much deeper levels of the subtle physiology. The deep circulation of *ch'i* is a process of internal alchemy through which the sexual fluid *(ching)* is transformed into vital energy *(ch'i)* and finally refined into spirit *(shen).*

Sexual energy, vital energy, and spiritual energy are only three aspects of a unified whole. The reason the Taoist sexual practitioner sought intercourse with throngs of young virgins is because sexual energy *(ching)* is at its peak during youth, when it is naturally transformed into vital *(ch'i)* and spiritual *(shen)* energies. The vitality and spiritual idealism of youth is based on an overflow of sexual energy. By association with young virgins the Taoist practitioner becomes irradiated with this energy and can transform it to still higher levels. After youth, however, the body does not produce as much sexual fluid or energy. Thus, if the vital and spiritual energies are not carefully preserved, they will suffer, resulting in ill health, disease, and death. By hoarding the *ching* and transforming it into *ch'i* and finally into *shen,* the normal aging process is reversed. Just as the deer accumulates vast amounts of energy by resting with his nose touching his tail, thereby creating an unbroken circle of flowing energy, so did the Taoists devise techniques of meditation to accelerate the natural transformation of sexual energies into vital and spiritual power. One of these methods was called the Greater Heavenly Circulation. In this meditation the attention is directed inward to the abdomen. A circular current of energy moves down to the sexual organs, up the spine to the brain, forward and downward along the face and chest, and then down to the abdomen. At first, the meditator visualizes the breath moving along with the current of energy, but eventually realizes that the circulation of this energy is spontaneous and experiences it as a current of heat. As this circulation continues, the energy becomes increasingly rarefied, especially when it reaches the head. Here it produces a great feeling of expansion and peace, then it condenses into a heavenly elixir and descends again into the abdomen. Finally, an elixir of luminous, liquid, golden light is formed in the head. It rains down into the "caldron" of the abdomen, where it crystallizes into an immortal "fetus" of light. At this point the fetus is capable of rising up the spine and emerging from the crown of the head. Those who have succeeded in this practice have a subtle nimbus above their heads. Like the deer, their sexual energy has accumulated in the head to the point of extrusion.

Chinese folklore is full of legends in which an Emperor or a hermit deep in the mountains is approached by a fairy who makes love with him. In fact, as we have seen, this is how the art of clouds and rain was taught to one of China's first Emperors. As the practice of inner sexuality developed, the internal circulation of energy was facilitated by visualizing a beautiful fairy-woman within one's own body and making love with her. Thus all the forces of yin and yang necessary to gain immortality are found within the human form. A fairy Goddess with a complexion as pure as jade is found within every man. The adept was advised to inhale her breath and contemplate her beauty. Through this internal sexuality the man would not have to have access to a harem of virgins. He would thus be self-sufficient in his quest for immortality. Nor would he have to fear the loss of his vitality to such damsels, for they were simply forms of his vital energy.

This art of inner sexuality grew so popular that Taoists would actually shun the advances of women. One story has it that a Taoist monk used to visit a beautiful young virgin, though he never made love with her. One night she drank a lot of plum wine and attempted to seduce him. He explained to her that the yin and yang within his body were already making love like a man and woman, and that this internal union was infinitely more satisfying than making love externally.

Finally, however, the Taoists developed a method that combined the virtues of making love both with a partner and internally. This method was known as "dual cultivation." Whereas the heterodox practices relied upon stimulation and exploitation of the woman, and involved considerable control on the part of the male, the art of dual cultivation was truly Taoist, as it involved surrender rather than manipulative sexual strategies. Rather than seeking to extract the fluids of the woman, the Taoist practitioner of dual cultivation sought to enter into increasingly subtle fields of vital and spiritual energy with her. The practice was based on bioelectrical and spiritual fields rather than on hydraulic engineering. Performed after midnight, dual cultivation requires that both partners abstain from rich food or wine. Otherwise their minds will be dull and their internal organs harmed. First, they must meditate. After their minds have become serene, they come together in silent, motionless intercourse. As fields of energy build up between them, they surrender to them, visualizing the flow of energy within their bodies. Neither the man nor the woman experiences genital orgasm. If this form of sex is performed for a long period, both partners will gain the strength of youth and achieve longevity.

Thus after a long period of sexual practices based on control and manipulation, a method of lovemaking evolved that was based on absorption into the field of dynamic stillness from which Taoism springs. Again, the softest and quietest had overcome the strongest and most active. As we will see in the next chapter, in India this subtle embrace was developed to a high degree.

Lotuses

*B*ATHED WITH SCENTED BREEZES from the Indian Ocean, the inner chamber of Ravana's palace is umbrellaed by a radiant swan-white canopy. Underneath, many women, dressed in finery, their fragrant hair adorned with garlands of flowers, are lying stretched out on ornate carpets. After spending half the night in amorous play, they are afloat in deep, wine-sweetened sleep. In its stillness this slumbering harem, covered with tinkling ornaments now fallen silent, is like a vast nocturnal pool blossoming with lotuses, with no sound of swans or humming of bees. The eyes and mouths of these lovely women are closed like lotus petals folded with night, awaiting the dawn to reopen. From them rises a fragrance like water lilies. The radiance of this harem is like the clear starry heavens of an autumn night, and Ravana shines amid them like the moon encircled by brilliant stars. The women glow like clusters of comets falling luminously through the firmament. Some have collapsed into slumber in the middle of a dance, lying as though stunned by a bolt of lightning, their hair in disarray and their jewelry scattered around them; others have let tinkling anklets fall from their feet and have smudged their makeup. Some have flung their garlands to the floor and, with broken strings of pearls, unclasped girdles, and skirts slipped back, look like unsaddled mares; still others, having lost earrings, their hazy garlands torn and trampled, look like flowering vines trodden down by wild elephants. Here and there moonbeams play among sleeping swans of breasts, reflected between strands of pearls rising and falling with their breaths. These women are rivers: their thighs, the shores; their bellies, rippling waters, their faces, golden lotuses; their amorous desires, crocodiles; their sensuous bodies, the riverbed. The little bells sewn on their silken gowns sound like rippling wavelets. On their ankles, necks, shoulders and wrists, bellies, and tips of the breasts they bear like ornaments purple love bruises and faint scratches, signs of where a lion or tiger has come to drink. The veils of some, rising and falling with their fragrant breath, flutter like iridescent flags, and their earrings, tinkling softly, are fanned by their scented breaths. Some of these women repeatedly savor each other's lips and tongue in their dreams, as if they are kissing their master. With passion aroused, these lovely, dreaming women make love with each other in their sleep; others with jewel-laden limbs embrace heaps of fine garments; even in sleep the dancers move sensuously, embracing like long-absent lovers drums and lutes. Some rest a head or limb on a companion's belly, or between her breasts, her thighs, or the small of her back; amorously entwined, these slender-waisted women couple like woven garlands of flowers opening with the breeze. As Ravana sleeps, the radiance of these women plays upon him like golden lamplight.

Thus reads one of the most famous passages of Indian literature. It is translated from the epic known as the *Ramayana* and amply demonstrates that the poets of India are lavish in their praise of women. With their tremulous eyes, darting and flashing like little minnows, their gazellelike eyes, their eyes like dark lotus blossoms—poison, ambrosial eyes; their alluring, high, close-set breasts, swelling, dark-nippled breasts; their undulant, golden-limbed bodies, nectarlike lips and mouths like mangoes; their smooth thighs, deep navels, and flowing hair massed like thick, blossoming, iridescent darkness, their midnight of hair and starlike strands of pearls; their breath fragrant as flowers of paradise and voices like sweet, tinkling bells, flowing softly as liquified moonlight—they flood the poetic imagination like celestial visions. In India sex, and especially the fairer sex, is divine. One has only to consider the institution of the temple prostitute in order to realize that divinity suffuses even the basest forms of sex. In medieval India, dancing girls acted as prostitutes at local temples. They became so in a ceremony in which they were married to the God of the temple. Part of a prostitute's wifely duties was to have intercourse with passing men. And her patrons, by making love with the God's wife, would thereby enter into communion with the divinity. Thus a sensual act, undertaken for pleasure, was also a divine ritual act for both prostitute and patrons.

Wherever we encounter a God or Goddess—in myth, in the voluptuous volumes of sculpture, in religious icons, or in the visions of saints—the divine image is always sensuously alluring and imbued with irresistible erotic appeal. Perhaps the most seductive of all is Krishna, the Dark One, the enchanting, blue-black God incarnate, bluer than blue water lilies. To the scholar he was a legendary hero of an ancient and sexually free tribal people. To the yogi sitting in meditation, he is the entire universe. To the village girls of Brindaban, his boyhood home, he is the naughty God incarnate who stole their clothes while they were bathing, and the object of their every desire. Originally the legend of Krishna was celebrated amid wanton sexual orgies. As the patriarchal Brahmans imposed their religion on the more sexually free matriarchal societies, however, the legend was incorporated into the Hindu scriptures. In this way passionate love was transformed from the realm of the flesh to the contemplation of a divine incarnation who wandered the earth as a young man, beholding the dark evening sky illumined by the moon. The air was fragrant with the perfume of lotuses, and the forests buzzed with clouds of swarming bees. In such a setting Krishna dreamed of making love with the local cowherd women. Singing in a low, pleasing voice, he allured these ladies with his beautiful song. They abandoned their homes and stole away in the dusk to be with their dark lover.

Hearing his voice, one woman sung along softly. Another simply dreamed of him. One whispered, "O Krishna, O Krishna!" under her breath. Another, blind with love, embraced him. Yet another stayed at home and, meditating on him with eyes closed, merged with him in the bliss of her heart.

Surrounded by these cowherd women, Krishna became eager to dance with them. Throngs of beautiful women, their limbs gracefully mimicking his gestures, swayed about, looking for him. Some cried out in rapture, "I am Lord Krishna! Behold my amorous movements!"

One cowherd lady studied the ground, then suddenly, with eyes opening like lotuses, cried, "I see Krishna's footprints. Some lucky girl has met with him; her small footprints are by his. Look, here he has plucked some high-growing flowers as his footprints show only the toes. Here a woman wanders distract-edly, having touched Krishna's hand, and then is abandoned by him."

Upon seeing this, the women were saddened and lost all hope of seeing Krishna. They wandered to the banks of the river and there saw Krishna, the protec-tor of the worlds. He made them all happy, speaking kindly and touching them with his hands. He danced with them and took each one of them by the hand in a huge circle. They would close their eyes at the touch of his hand and hear only the tinkling of his bracelets.

Krishna sang of the moonlight, the lotuses, and the autumn, but the cowherd women sang only of Krishna. He danced with each woman, and a moment without him seemed like a thousand years.

Once on a spring night, the moon was full. The woods were fragrant with the perfume of jasmine and the cuckoos were singing. The ground was strewn with silken garments perfumed with musk and sandal-wood. Couches for love play were positioned about. Jeweled lamps lit the scene. Krishna played his flute to arouse the desires of the ladies, who had stolen away from their husbands' beds. Seeing his sweet-heart, Radha, he glanced at her. Embracing her they retired to a lovely bed of love and made love in eight postures. Assuming other forms, Krishna embraced all the lusty cowherd women and made love to them all simultaneously. Then he danced with them once again, changing into many forms and stealing their hearts. Then he made love with them all again amid the tin-

kling of bracelets and anklets. As they all climaxed, a
cry rose up from them, they all fainted in unison. Then
they fell silent and goosebumps covered their limbs.
Their braids were disheveled, their skirts loosened,
their upper garments discarded. As Krishna made love
with every one simultaneously, in sixteen postures, all
the Gods and their lovely consorts arrived on golden
chariots, watching delightedly. Struck by the arrows
of love, the women's bodies shivered all over. In thirty-
three sylvan groves, the Dark One made passionate
love with thirty-three women for thirty-three days
without satisfying their desires. Their passion only
blazed higher and more furiously, like fires fed with
clarified butter. In India, divinity is sexy.

The followers of the cult of Krishna, however, feel
that all souls are feminine with respect to God.
Therefore, male devotees often live, act, and dress like
women so that they might cultivate the emotion of
devotional surrender to their lover, Krishna. Such
devotees are still found in India. However, they do
not display the prim dress and pious mannerisms of
nuns, but act like gay, flirtatious girls, arrayed in silken
saris and tinkling bracelets and anklets. They giggle
and blush and often live among women so that they
might more easily learn the attitude of devotion.

Other worshipers of Krishna formed couples. They
would stimulate intense, even violent, erotic emotions in themselves by reading and chanting the amorous adventures of their God. Then they would
perform sexual yoga, in which the male would play
the part of Krishna and his partner, the role of one of
the cowherd girls. Love rituals were performed in large
circles. It was felt that more intense erotic emotion
could be produced if the women in such rituals were
the wives of other men. After all, Krishna himself had

hundreds of sexual partners who were the wives of others. Girls highly trained in the skill of love were greatly prized in these circles.

Many scholars feel that the cult of courtly love in the West was inspired by the cult of Krishna. Our modern obsession with the unattainable object of romantic love has much in common with the quest for a transcendental lover; and the Hare Krishna advocates we find at our airports seem to have brought the movement full circle.

One of India's earliest scriptures, *The Great Forest Teaching*, tells us that the entire universe arose from copulation. In the beginning there was only the Supreme Being, existing all alone. With omniscient vision he looked in all directions but could find nothing but himself. He had no delight. Therefore, he desired another. He divided himself in two, like a man and woman making love. From this division arose husband and wife. He made love with her, and human beings were produced. She decided to play hide-and-seek, and transformed herself into a cow. He became a bull and copulated with her. Thus cattle were born. She became a mare and he, a stallion. Thus horses were born. She became a she-ass and he, a he-ass. Thus single-hoofed animals were born. She became a she-goat, he a he-goat; she a ewe, he a ram. From this union goats and sheep were born. Thus he begat all couples and the whole universe. In short, the Supreme Being, for the sake of delight, copulated with an endless array of female forms like a bull among his herd. Likewise, the hero who died in battle or the celibate yogi who went to Heaven could look forward to erotic dalliance with troupes of radiant celestial nymphs. It was part of a man's duty on earth to imitate these divine practices. Thus the wildest male

fantasies recieved divine sanction. From the viewpoint of the Indian male, the ideal household contained numerous wives, concubines, maids, musicians,
and dancers, all eager to please their husband
and master who played among them like a radiant
God.

Ancient India was not the parched, poverty-
stricken, and deforested land it now is. Its resplendent, fortified cities once towered like monuments in
what was perhaps the fairest landscape there has ever
been. In this land were lush gardens with ponds of
lotus, bristling with swelling buds, where lovers tar-
ried in pleasure pavilions. At dusk these parks grew
wild with song, dance, and more private pastimes, especially in spring when the nights grew shorter and
the days, which used to lie curled up, began to stretch
out their limbs. In this season the mango-anointed
breezes pierced the hearts of young ladies and young
men separated from their lovers. Beautiful courtesans, female dancers, poets, and musicians employed
by rulers gladdened these parks with their presence.
For in ancient India women were not secluded, but
moved freely in a society where matriarchal traditions were still strong. Premarital love and extramar-
ital sex were common. Although a woman might feign
modesty before her lover, unable to guard her un-
veiled bosom with her slender arms, she would be the
first to make all things possible, tossing the lotus from
her hair at the candle and puffing out its shaken flame.
And once modesty was overcome in the dark, she
would often take the active role to fulfill the desires
of her body and soul.

These courtesans were the earthly counterparts of
heavenly damsels and were expert in the rite of passion. Their supple bodies were a highly desirable
erotic asset; and many courtesans were so flexible that,

standing on their feet, they could arch over backward then, resting on their forearms, eat fruit off the floor with their lips. They longed to enjoy every posture in the art of love, frequently engaging in an encyclopedic display of sexual choreography. Indian mathematicians of the era often attempted to calculate the possible combinations and permutations of coital acrobatics, the most fertile mind imagining only some seven hundred. As we shall see, Gods were capable of dreaming up many times that number. These agile courtesans, many of them skilled in dance and yoga, moved in the art of love like undulant swells— a storm surf mounting with graceful exercise of each new mystery. Should a woman's lover retreat before the storm reached its full fury, she would cast at him dark, sidelong glances, flashing with frustrated passion. For women were thoroughly versed in the erotic arts and expected as much from their lovers. A cultured woman was expected to have a sound knowledge of sixty-four auxiliary arts in order to be considered a good lover. These talents included singing, playing musical instruments, dancing, painting, decorating one's forehead, the art of adorning an idol with rice and flowers, flower arranging, bed making, garland weaving, the art of designing earrings and other ornaments, the art of mixing perfumes for the skin in order to stimulate sexual desire, the art of dressing tastefully, magic and sleight of hand, cooking, the preparation of sherbets and other beverages, sewing, the solution of riddles, the art of reciting verses in a game between lovers, mimicry, reasoning and logic, chanting, fencing, carpentry, gardening, teaching parrots to speak, composing poems, and the art of sizing up a man in a glance. A woman versed in these arts· was much sought after, for her skills enriched courtly sexual dalliance with an aura of idle opulence reminiscent of the sensuous delights of the Gods.

However mystical they may be, Indians are fond of analysis. In the texts concerning the erotic arts, they list categories of human sexual types; various kinds of men and women; the sexual characteristics of women from different regions of India; the flow of erotic sensations to different zones in a woman's body during the stages of the lunar cycle; every conceivable posture, embrace, kiss, scratch, blow or bite; instructions for wooing a new bride, a stranger, another man's wife; and how to prepare aphrodisiacs.

The most desirable type of woman was known as the Padami, or Lotus Woman, who is said to have descended from the realm of the Gods. She has a radiant, moonlike countenance, fawn eyes, full and elevated breasts, a thin waist, and three folds of skin at her navel. Her melodious voice, golden complexion, and refinement make her highly desirable. Her vagina is perfumed like a lotus blossom. She likes to make love during the daytime.

The next most desirable woman is the Chitini, or Art Woman. She is less spiritual than the Lotus Woman, though both dislike violence in love. She, too, is full-breasted but has larger thighs than the Lotus Woman. She walks with the swinging gait of an elephant and is fond of the arts. Her secretions smell like honey, and she prefers to make love at night.

The Shankini, or Conch Woman, is not very beautiful. She is either too thin, too tall, or too fat. She has a thick waist, small breasts, and a harsh voice. She likes violence in sex, and often leaves nailmarks on her lover. Her vagina is salty, and she likes to make love at night.

Last, the Hastini, or Elephant Woman, is considered the lowest sexual type. She should be avoided entirely by men of refined taste. She is slow, even sluggish, and stout. Her vagina is pungent, like that of an elephant. She craves love at any hour.

Likewise, there are four types of men. The manly, good-looking, and altruistic Hare Man is suited to the Lotus Woman. The warriorlike, chivalrous Buck Man is right for the Art Woman. The rough-and-ready Bull Man is best for the Conch Woman; and the ugly, coarse, and lustful Stallion Man is fit for the Elephant Woman.

This fourfold division of men and women corresponds to the four castes. The Lotus Woman and Hare Man correspond to the spiritual Brahmans. The Art Woman and her Buck lover belong to the strong warrior caste. The Conch Woman and Bull Man correspond to the merchant caste; and the Elephant Woman and Stallion Man belong to the coarse agricultural caste.

The spiritually fragrant love of a Lotus Woman would be entirely lost on a male with coarser qualities. Whereas the Elephant Woman should be tackled only by a Stallion Man, the Lotus Woman and Hare Man are capable of a contemplative and spiritual union.

The reason for this classification lies deep in the Indian experience of life, for they see all creation as a flowing stream. Objects are like whirlpools in a river, ever changing with the waters that stream through them. The stream of life flowing through Brahmans is spiritual and should include food, music, marriage partners, and activities of a spiritual nature. The currents of life streaming through warriors, merchants, and agriculturalists are thought to be of an increasingly debased, darker quality. A Brahman devotes his time not to fighting, or to getting and spending, but to meditation and teaching. If one sits and listens to a spiritual person deliver a lecture, it is believed that the latter's "vibrations" actually flow through the audience, altering the substance of one's life. The reason Indian gurus never engage in dialogue is because they would be receiving a flow of vibrations from lesser beings. Their role is to give of their pure substance by lecturing practically uninterruptedly to inferior beings.

The sexual arts teach that first of all lovers should be sensitive to the vibrational field of which they are a part and find a suitable match. Not every Brahman female may look like a beautiful Lotus Woman, but she is supposed to have spiritual qualities. There is a subtle implication in the erotic texts that whoever has spiritual qualities is a Lotus Woman or Hare Man, despite her or his caste designation. Yet, what if a woman and a man are of a harmonious degree of vibrational refinement but the sizes of their sexual organs are unevenly matched? Meditation on this problem gave rise to the classification of men and women according to sexual dimensions and the enumeration of all the possible and desirable combinations. In general, a High Union is between a man and a woman whose sexual proportions are slightly inferior to his. Should she be very much smaller than he, this would constitute a Very High Union. A Low Union is formed when the female's dimensions are much larger than the male's.

Having found a lover of harmonious temperament and suitable size, a man well versed in the erotic arts will stimulate his lover with kisses and caresses on erogenous zones of her body that shift in sensitivity with the phases of the moon cycle. Beginning at the full moon, the sensitivity descends from the forehead through the eyes, then down the left side of the body through the cheeks, lips, neck, shoulder, armpit, breast, hip, genitals, knee, ankle and foot. At the new moon, the sensitivity ascends the right side of the body, arriving at the head and hair at the time of the full moon. The ancient texts state that this shift takes place because of the varying degrees of light and darkness during the lunar cycle. Modern scientific evidence confirms this schema to a degree, for the two major glands in the head, the pineal and the pituitary, which secrete hormones that influence one's whole physiology, are activated by light. Women are especially sensitive to the lunar cycle, which affects not only their physiology but also delicate emotional states. Keeping this in mind, we can begin to appreciate the degree of subtlety the science of *eros* achieved in ancient India. Although attempting to incite pleasure in a woman from the big toe upward by following the phases of the moon may seem to be taking the matter too far, many a Western woman would surely welcome a map of erogenous zones that is not confined to the lips, breasts, and vagina. And it is interesting that at a time when the Christian church was compiling an encyclopedia of sins, the Indians were listing an encyclopedia of pleasures.

In ancient India the physical aspect of sex is always related and subordinate to a larger, subtler, and more powerful energy field, whether it is the level of refinement at which a lover vibrates, the influence of the lunar cycle, or underlying emotions. Therefore, the varieties of embraces and lovemaking postures indicated by the ancient sages of love are never mere physical acts, but are always suffused with emotion, from violent erotic abandon to serene spiritual surrender. Under the right conditions, holding hands can contain as much as or more emotion than full sexual intercourse. People familiar with yoga, mime, or the martial or dramatic arts will know that psychological states seem to arise that are specific to particular bodily postures. India has, through the practice of yoga and meditation, produced something of a science of the emotions. The highest emotion is the attitude of divine love, which often involves sexual intercourse in specific bodily postures. Many of the temple prostitutes married to the God Vishnu were also skilled in dance and yoga. As mentioned above, part of a prostitute's duties as the deity's wife involved ritual intercourse with strangers. By adopting the yoga positions of the fish, the tortoise, the wheel, and the seashell in succession during lovemaking, a prostitute performed a dance in which the first four incarnations of her God and husband, Vishnu, are ritually embodied. Her client thus unites with forms of the deity while she ritually *becomes* them.

In a more secular area, if a woman clings to her lover's body like a creeping vine climbing around a tree trunk, with only one leg raised and wrapped around his thigh, she does so in order to express or intensify a particular emotion welling up within her. The physical form of the embrace is as intimately intertwined with the invisible emotional field she is absorbed in as her body is with her lover's. While it is true that some women are definitely brought to orgasm more easily in some erotic positions than others, it would be a mistake to assume that this was the sole purpose of these poses. Quite the opposite. Indian erotics emphasize the pursuit and prolongation of preorgasmic pleasure rather than the quick production of orgasm. Assuming a number of poses in a single session has the effect of directing erotic sensation away from the genitals, lessening genital tension and thus the demand for orgasm. In this way every area of the body was bathed in highly charged erotic energy. Many of the positions are used in yoga to divert sexual energy away from the genitals to higher glandular functions. Thus sex could serve as a form of yoga leading to divine communion.

Of course, sentiments other than ecstasy, even violent ones, arise during sex; and the Indian bedroom arts allowed for these in no small degree. The woman is encouraged to be as aggressive as the man and even to dominate him. Female superior positions are forbidden in many cultures on moral or religious grounds, often simply to preserve the dignity of men who must maintain a sense of domination. In Indian erotics such positions are not only permitted but highly lauded, because this is the way Goddesses make love with their Gods and therefore they are dignified enough for mere mortals.

Indian bedroom arts also include room for pain, physical and mental, as a stimulator of passion. Petty quarrels followed by passionate reconciliation, and exquisite wounds inflicted by nails, lips, and teeth, followed by tender kisses and caresses, add dynamism to romance and allow lovers to act out aggressions in a playful way. Scratching and titillating a woman with the nails can be done lightly until the hairs on her body rise and a shudder passes over all her limbs. One technique, the Peacock's Foot, is made by placing the ball of the thumb upon her nipple and pressing the four remaining fingers on the soft white part of the breast, leaving a mark like a peacock's claw. Such marks should be made with more pressure when the woman is angry or when her lover is going to separate from her for a period of time. First of all, the strong pressure of the fingers will stimulate her to discharge her blocked anger; second it will leave lasting marks that will make the lovers remember each other with fondness while one or the other is away. In the same way, ornamental marks can be made with the teeth that will kindle hot desire and leave a lingering emotional impression each time they are admired in the mirror. Even soft tapping and hammering with the hands are encouraged.

What is most touching in Indian erotics is the exceeding tenderness of the man's approach to his lover. Just as the sequence of postures and embraces assumed during a love bout are but visible forms of subtle emotional and spiritual states, the stages of courtship proceed delicately in accordance with a woman's signs of interest. Again, the physical acts are secondary to the emotional field present between the lovers.

Half-innocent smiles, oblique, hurried glances, a quavering voice, slight inflections of the brow, sentiments hovering close to love but still denying it—such are the indications that a young woman has reached the age when her heart is torn between fear and curiosity, bashfulness and desire, and is no longer pure and simple. Each of her limbs is softened at adolescence and seems to swim in a sea of beauty. The elements of hardness gather only at her budding breasts. At the sight of such steep breasts, deep navel, and shifting glances, what young man could fail to stumble?

He spies her at picnics and festivals. She stretches. Her arms are raised voluptously, as she listens to the love adventures of older, more daring women. He spies her afterward, acting out her new knowledge to a crowd of admiring younger friends. Or he catches her with mirror in hand, admiring her reflection, training her mouth in little smiles, exploring new expressions with her eyebrows, and perfecting sidelong glances which she suddenly casts at him in its reflection. These, too, indicate that she is losing interest in dolls and toys in favor of other forms of play. But how is he to know that she is interested in him? The love of a young woman is betrayed by certain outward signs. She blushes when he gazes upon her, and she turns her head away. She invents some pretext to show him her ankles, arms, and legs. She steals glances at him while his back is turned and hangs her head when he asks her a question, answering indistinctly. She takes delight in his company, and tells him long tales, very slowly, never wanting the conversation to end. She hugs and kisses a child in his presence, and always wears rings and other ornaments he may have presented her.

Having seen these signs of affection for him, a young man should do everything possible to win her over entirely. When playing sports or games together, he should take every opportunity to touch her hand. When alone he should embrace her in many ways. When swimming he should dive at a distance, surfacing near her so that their damp bodies touch. He should appear poetically affected at the sight of spring leaves and budding flowers. He should describe to her the torments of love he endures.

At parties and festivals, he should sit near her, touching her secretly, and placing his foot upon hers, slowly touch each of her toes. He should then caress her foot with his hand, stroking it gently. Whenever he is with her, he should express his passion in all his gestures and acts.

If she seems receptive, he should indicate he has

something very private to tell her and, taking her to a quiet, romantic place, should express his love more by gentle caresses than by words. When he is sure of her feelings for him, he should pretend to be ill and ask her to come visit him. When she arrives he should take her hand, place it on his brow, and ask her to prepare some medicine for him, saying, "It is you, and no one else, who must do this for me." When she leaves he should ask her to return the next day. This pretended illness should last two or three days. Thus she will be accustomed to coming to his house, and he can then have long conversations with her. For no matter how much he loves her he will not win her over without a great deal of pleasant conversation.

The sages of Indian erotics advise that a man should gain the confidence of a young virgin slowly, for women have gentle natures and want tender beginnings. If they are forcibly approached by men, they may develop a hatred of sex and of men in general. A man should therefore approach a woman with gentleness and tenderness, according to her desire. Soon she will no longer be afraid and will have confidence in him.

He should kiss her the first time in the manner most pleasing to her, but it should be very short, a mere invitation. He should then embrace only the upper part of her body. If the woman is mature and has known the man for some time, he may embrace her by lamplight. But if she is a young girl or he hardly knows her, then he should embrace her in darkness. He should put a piece of fruit in her mouth, then kiss her gently. Gradually he should touch her breasts, and if she stops him, should say, "I will stop only if you kiss me again." Following this, he should embrace her once again, letting his hands wander all over her body with gradually increasing pressure. If she still backs away, he should tease her saying he will bite and scratch her so hard that it will leave marks all over her body. And he says that he will do the same to his own body and will tell all her friends she did it. Thus, by being alternately excited and calmed, her confidence will grow along with her passion.

When she grows less timid, he should caress and kiss her all over, and gently slide his hands onto her thigh where it joins her torso. If she objects, he should ask, "What harm is there in doing this?" Then he should gently touch her most sensitive and private parts, undo her dress, and caress her naked thighs. All these things must be done with subtlety and gentleness, but he should not yet begin intercourse. Finally, he should tell her how much he loves her, then have intercourse with her. Thus he should not follow her whims blindly or constantly oppose her, but adopt a middle course. If he neglects a girl, thinking her too bashful, she will think him a beast, ignorant of how to conquer a woman.

The sages advised that older, more experienced women require less coaching. However, a man needs special knowledge to approach a married woman. Adultery in ancient India was taken for granted, and coolly calculated instructions are given for seducing another man's wife—and in some instances, the sages say, adultery might even save a man's life. For the intensity of a man's desire for a woman increases by degree, beginning with an attraction of the eye, and continuing with an attachment of the mind, a loss of sleep, bodily emanciation, a turning away from objects of enjoyment, a shameless disregard for modesty and prudence, madness, fainting, and finally death. Given such eventualities, seduction is the only alternative.

But ancient India, where love was sensuous, happy,

and free, is not modern India. Gradually rules and moral restraints multiplied and grew tighter. Women no longer roamed about freely, and a chastely married wife became the model woman. Passionate, sensuous India perished in favor of the idea of faithful devotion.

Upward-Flowing Semen

India has always been a land of unrestrained extremes. Summer wilts and burns the vegetation, drying up lakes and swamplands. In the hot dust, water buffaloes shake their horns trying to drive away busy swarms of gnats from their bloodshot eyes. In June everything changes. The monsoons sweep over most of the continent like a fertilizing God. The earth, parched and cracked open with the heat, suddenly begins to feel the cool balm of easterly winds. Confused masses of torpid cumulus clouds seethe on the horizon, building into huge thunderheads. The sky blackens and opens up with such devastating power that the pouring water seems solid rather than moving. Nights are deep; thick clouds obscure the moon and stars, and the darkness seems even darker when interrupted by flashes of lightning. Women hurry through the downpour to meet with their lovers, their thin rain-soaked saris clinging transparently to their breasts. Lovers stay in bed all day. Embracing their dark women, holding them breast to breast, the men make love to the sound of the rumbling downpour. The riverbanks overflow, and schools of fish, bright as coins, dart over what yesterday was dust.

Making love amid the monsoons is merely adding

a human accompaniment to a divine fertility rite. For rain in ancient India was the seed of the Gods. The outflow of human semen into the womb was an imitation of this divine, primordial act. The climate of celestial sensuality in early Indian court life attests to this. But there was always a countervailing tendency. While a young prince would gather his five favorite wives about him and make love to all simultaneously, using his toes, fingers, and penis, a yogi would sit in the center of five blazing fires, driving his five senses inward, his semen drawn up like a flame of rainbow arching high over coal-dark clouds.

Such a yogi is said to have "upward-flowing" semen. The semen is never discharged but drawn up into the organism to nourish the entire nervous and hormonal systems. The powers and pleasures derived from such celibacy are thought to be enormous. Along with fasting, observing silence, and other austerities, celibacy generates a kind of heat in the body and soul known as *tapas*. *Tapas* creates so much power in a yogi that nothing in Heaven or on earth is beyond his attainment. Even the Gods fear such a holy one. Indra, the King of Gods, thinking that he will be dethroned by such a yogi, sends indescribably beautiful heavenly nymphs down to earth to seduce him and exhaust his store of semen and *tapas*. One such yogi was the seer named Kaṇḍu. His story reveals much concerning the dynamics of upward-flowing semen.

"On the lovely, deserted and sanctifying bank of the river Gomatī, full of bulbs, roots and fruits, of kindling, flowers and *kuśa* grass, covered with all kinds of trees and creepers, and adorned with many blossoms, resonant with many birds, enchanting and grazed by various herds of deer, there stood the hermitage of Kaṇḍu, rich at all seasons in fruits and flowers and adorned with a stand of plantain trees. There the seer did great and marvelous *tapas*, with vows, fasts, restraints and the observances of baths and silence: in summer he sat surrounded by the five fires; in the rainy season he stayed outdoors; in winter he stayed immersed in the river up to his chin. Thus did he mortify himself.

"The Gods became greatly amazed at the spectacle of the prowess of the hermit's *tapas*. With the force of his *tapas* Kaṇḍu heated up the three worlds of earth, atmosphere and heaven. 'Aho, what fortitude! Aho, what extreme *tapas!*' exclaimed the Gods.

"They diligently took counsel with Indra, upset from fear of Kaṇḍu, seeking to obstruct his *tapas*. Knowing their purpose, Indra, the Slayer of Vala, spoke to the callipygous heavenly nymph Pramloca, who was proud of her beauty and youth. She was fine-waisted, with beautiful teeth, full hips and ample breasts, and endowed with all the fine marks of beauty. 'Pramloca, go quickly where that hermit is doing *tapas* and seduce him, my pretty, to deplete his power of *tapas*.' Said Pramloca, 'I always obey your words, my lord, chief of the Gods, but here I am afraid that I will risk my life. I am afraid of this great hermit who observes the vow of celibacy; he is awesome with the fire of his *tapas* and his glow is like fire and sun. Knowing that I have come to obstruct him, Kaṇḍu will be angry, and that extremely powerful man will lay an unendurable curse on me. There are many other celestial nymphs who take pride in their beauty and youth, who have fine waists and pretty faces and big uptilted bosoms, and who are adept at seduction—put them to the task!'

"Indra replied to her words, 'Let the others be; you

are the most skilled, my lovely! I shall give you Love, Spring and Wind to help you. Go with them, fine-hipped girl, to that great hermit.'

"Hearing Indra's command, that lovely-eyed nymph went off with the others by way of the sky. When she arrived there, she saw that charming wood and the fiercely practicing and taintless hermit in his hermitage. . . . Slowly she strolled with the others through the woods, and beholding its charms and marvels the beautiful woman opened her eyes wide in wonderment. Pramloca said to Wind, Love and Spring, 'Help me out! Each of you be ready!' and confident of her powers of seduction she added, 'I shall now go where that hermit is keeping himself. Today I shall change that driver of his body who has harnessed the horses of his senses into a poor charioteer whose reins are slipping, at the command of lust! Be he Brahmā, Vishnu or Shiva, today I shall lay him open to the wounds of the arrows of love!' With these words she proceeded to the hermit's hermitage, where the wild beasts were tamed by the power of his *tapas*.

"She positioned herself on the river's bank and at a short distance from him the beautiful nymph began to sing as sweetly as the cuckoo. Thereupon Spring quickly displayed its power, and out of season the cuckoos began to sing enticingly. Wind blew the fragrance of the sandal woods of Mt. Malaya, ever so slowly dropping all kinds of pure flowers. Love approached carrying his blossom arrows and disturbed the thoughts of the seer.

"When he heard the music of her song, the hermit wonderingly ventured out, propelled by the arrows of Love, to where the fine-browed nymph was standing. Seeing her he said happily, his eyes wide with wonder, his robe drooping, staggering, his body covered with goosebumps, 'Who are you and who do you belong to, you fine-hipped, lovable, sweet-smiling wench? You are stealing my heart, lovely-brows! Quick, tell me the truth, slim-waisted girl.'

"Said Pramloca, 'I am your serving girl; I have come here for flowers. Give me your orders now: what are you telling me to do?' Scarcely had he heard her words before he lost his composure. Bewildered, he took the woman by the hand and entered the hermitage. Love, Wind and Spring went back to heaven, satisifed they had done their duty. They went to Indra and told him what had happened between the two of them. Upon hearing this, Indra and the Gods were pleased and relieved.

"Kaṇḍu meanwhile had entered his hermitage with Pramloca, and by the power of his *tapas* gave himself at once the handsome, lovable body of a sixteen-year-old, endowed with beauty and youth, most enticing, adorned with divine ornaments, wearing celestial robes, desirable, made up with divine garlands and perfumes fit for all pleasures. When she saw his fine manhood, she was amazed and delighted, exclaiming, 'Aho, the power of *tapas*.'

"He gave up bathing, worshiping the dawn, praying, offering oblations, studying, adoring the Gods, keeping vows, fasts and observances and meditating, and happily made love to her day and night. His heart smitten with love, he did not realize that he was losing *tapas*. So addicted did he become that he forgot dawn, night, day, fortnight, month, season, half-year and year, in fact all time, while the fine-hipped nymph, skilled in the moods of love as well as conversation, made love with him.

"Hermit Kaṇḍu stayed with her for over a hundred years, indulging his lusts. Then she said to the great man, 'I want to go back to heaven, brahmin.' The hermit, who was still in love with her, replied, 'Stay a few more days!' At his words the slender woman remained for another whole century, indulging in pleasure with the great-souled man.

" 'Give me leave, reverend, I am going to heaven,' she pleaded.

" 'No, stay!' he replied, so the lovely-faced nymph stayed another century.

" 'I am going to heaven, brahmin!' she stated with a pretty, affectionate smile, but he replied to the long-eyed woman, 'You remain with me here, fine-browed girl. You are not going for a long while.' Fearful of his curse, the fine-buttocked nymph stayed on for a little under two hundred years. Time and again the slender woman prayed him for leave to return to Indra's heaven, but every time the lordly man said, 'Stay!' Out of fear of his curse, but being also clever and aware of the grief from loss of affection, she did not leave the hermit. And when the great seer made love to her day and night, love was forever fresh to the lustful hermit.

"Then, one day, the hermit left his hut in a great hurry and the lovely nymph asked, 'Where are you going?'

" 'The day is ending and I have to worship the twilight; otherwise I am remiss in my rites.'

"She began to laugh cheerfully and said to the great hermit, 'How is it that only now the day is ending for you, O sage in all Dharma? It is long gone! Who would not be astounded at what you say?' Said the hermit, 'This morning you came to this lovely river bank, my dear. I saw you and you entered my hermitage. Now it is twilight and the day is drawing to a close. Why are you jesting? Tell me what you mean!'

"Pramloca said, 'True enough, I came in the morning, but centuries have passed since then!'

"Disturbed, the hermit asked the long-eyed woman, 'Tell me, timid thing, how much time have I spent dallying with you?'

"Pramloca said, 'Sixteen hundred years, six months and three days have gone by.'

"Said the seer, 'Are you telling the truth, or is this a joke, my lovely? I thought I had not been with you for more than a day!'

"Pramloca answered, 'Why should I lie to you, especially since you are asking me as you leave?'

"When the hermit heard her words, he cried, 'Fie! Fie on me!' and berated himself for his misconduct. 'All my *tapas* is lost! The wealth of the knowers of Truth has been dissipated; my wits are robbed! Someone has created woman to befuddle! By my conquest of myself I had knowledge of the highest Truth! A curse on this shark called lust which made me go this way! Vows, all the Scriptures and all other means of salvation have been destroyed by desire, which is the road to all hells.'

"Thus blaming himself, the hermit, wise in Dharma, said to the sitting nymph, 'Go where you want, slut! You have done what you had to do for Indra, shaking me up with the gestures of love. I won't reduce you to ashes in the fire of my wrath. I have lived with you in the friendship of the seven steps which the strict observe. But where are you to blame? What have I done for you? It is my fault entirely that I lost mastery over my senses. Still fie on you, disgusting seductress, for destroying my *tapas* as a favor to Indra!'

"While the brahmin seer was speaking in this vein to the fine-waisted nymph, she broke out in a sweat and trembled all over. And to the sweating and shivering woman that best of seers said irately, 'Now go! Go!' Tongue-lashed, she hurried out of the hermitage and flew into the air, wiping away her sweat with tree blossoms."[8]

Thus ends the tale of Kaṇḍu.

Episodes such as this provide one of the most common themes in Indian literature, and demonstrate that spirituality and sex are but two different expressions of heat that can change form as easily as a radiant hermit transforms his body into that of a handsome youth. Chastity culminates in desire, and fulfilled desire leads again to chastity. In India, remember, sex is always divine. The bliss of sexual union is no different than the timeless bliss of the Gods. The glowing rapture of the yogi is as erotic as the love play of a Goddess.

Semen, the fuel of both physical and spiritual bliss in the male, is not considered primarily a substance in Indian thought, but a process, a motion. It is the heated rush of ejaculation that creates sexual bliss and the serene upward flow of semen in the subtle physiology that affords spiritual rapture. Traditional Indian medical texts insist that retention of semen promotes longevity. A man's health and spiritual power thus depend on keeping in his seed. Females are believed to have a far greater store of spiritual power, and acquire even more during intercourse by absorbing their partner's semen through the vaginal wall.

If semen is lost during a nocturnal emission, the Indian scriptures advise that the seed be taken up with the thumb and fourth finger and rubbed between the breasts and the eyebrows. In this way even the semen that has fallen is moved upward toward the brain. The highest point the semen can attain is the crown of the head; and the masses of long hair piled up on the heads of yogis and Gods signify that their entire bodies are bursting with semen and an abundance of divine energy. In fact, one great Hindu saint, who was attacked by robbers and cut by a sword, bled semen (as the tale goes) rather than blood.

Anyone with the vaguest notion of Western physiology knows that the physical substance known as semen cannot fill the entire body, ascend the spinal column, and arrive in the brain. However, the Indian sages and the Taoists are not making a physiological mistake, but expressing a concept of the human body and its substances and processes that is based on their spiritual experience. In India, in the sexual or spiritual realm, the body is not considered a mere collection of cells, but an instrument of knowledge. Cognition of the most blissful forms of experience requires a healthy, finely tuned organism. From this viewpoint the semen is a source of light and is often equated with the sun, or Solar Semen, the creator of the entire universe. When a human emits semen into a womb, it is really the sun that is ejaculating, say the ancient scriptures. Furthermore, this solar light is identified with the immortal spirit within the human heart. Those yogis who experience the truth see the solar spirit sheathed in brilliant haloes of light. The Gods themselves are essentially made of this light, being more radiant than the sun and moon. From the heads of Hindu yogis and saints a flame ascends and envelops their bodies with a nimbus of light. All this luminosity is possible because of the light-generating power of the semen.

Luminosity is the semen's natural and original state, but when passion arises it becomes "darker," building lustily like storm clouds where before it had been flaming upward luminously. Finally, at the moment of orgasm, it pours downward and outward. In order to prevent this outflow, religious ascetics in India developed a literature of propaganda against the body and against females in particular. Probably the most memorable passage from this literature tells us that when the young prince who was to become the future Buddha renounced the world, he cast one last backward glance at his harem. The passage describing the women is based on the passage from the *Ramayana* at the opening of this chapter. But it has a different tone:

Richly dressed, these beautiful nymphs have fallen asleep. Their musical instruments are scattered about, fallen from their hands. One lies with her drum, embracing it like a lover, saliva drooling from her gaping mouth. Another, deep in sleep, grinds her teeth. Many mutter talk in their sleep, snoring with open mouths. Their dresses have fallen open, exposing their loathsome nakedness. They lie as if dead, as though having been crushed by an elephant and dropped. They seem like a lake of lotuses broken by the wind.

Thus the renunciation of the world begins with the depreciation of women.

We have, then, in India two extremes, never repressed but carried out to their farthest limits. One extreme is the generous and sensuous indulgence in erotic energy of early court life, a legacy of matriarchal tribal societies. The other is the niggardly hoarding of semen and the accumulation of spiritual power, a legacy of Hindu spiritualism. The task of the Indian mind was to create a myth, an art, a sexuality, and a spirituality that embrace these extremes.

The mythological creature most fully embodying these extremes is the God Shiva. Portrayed as an ascetic yogi, in meditation he is as immovable as a mountain. He sits amid the Himalayan peaks, his body smeared with the ashes of burned corpses. His semen is flowing ever upward in a pillar of fiery light that extends through the entire universe. This pillar of light forms an axis joining Heaven and earth. Thick, matted locks are massed atop his head, and contain so much transmuted sexual energy that the twisting blue waves of the Ganges River fall in vast cascades from them. He has a third eye in his forehead from which he can shoot flames generated by the ripe heat of his ascetic practices.

Once, the God of Erotic Love, attended by the spring breeze and a beautiful Goddess, the daughter of the Himalayas, went to the mountain hermitage of Shiva in order to make him fall in love. Only a son fathered by Shiva could save the world from the terror of a demon. They found Shiva deep in the bliss of meditation. The God of Love then shot an arrow at Shiva, but from the God's third eye flashed forth an incandescent arrow of fire, utterly consuming the God of Erotic Love. Clearly, Shiva is one who takes his celibacy seriously.

Yet he is the sexual libertine par excellence. He ended up marrying the beautiful Goddess. Her swelling breasts are like the temples of an elephant and from her tight embrace with him her body is covered with ashes. Although he makes love with her eternally, he never emits semen, since he has burnt with his *tapas* the God of Erotic Love. On the stony shores of a pure mountain lake he sits, seemingly in meditation, but he is actually inventing the 84,000,000 sexual postures. Only 84,000 has he taught to men, of which 729 are possible, given block and tackle. Or he enters the holy Pine Forest where great saints, living with their wives, perform deep meditation. When the lotus-eyed wives and comely daughters see Shiva, however, their minds become agitated, and lost in love, their senses burning with passion, they follow him about like elephant cows pursuing a bull. He dances like a wild man and copulates with them freely.

Ironically, celibate yogis have great potency in the very sexual activities they have renounced. One story tells of a woman burning with so much love that she could find no man to satisfy her. She disrobed, swearing that she would prowl the world naked until she met her match. The beautiful woman entered the hall of a great king. There were many men in the hall, including a yogi. She looked at the crowd, saying that there was not a real man in the room. The yogi bowed to the woman and took her home with him. There he made love with her so skillfully that, fatigued from repeated orgasms, she cried for mercy. The sexual power of Shiva is even greater. The king of the yogis, his semen flowing eternally upward, drawn by the force fields of his yogic quiescence, Shiva is also the master lover, able to make love eternally with his Goddess because his semen never falls. In fact, his endless amorous dalliance only stimulates his energy further, causing it to ascend ever more forcefully.

A potent visual image of Shiva's power is the *lingam,* or phallic icon, worshiped throughout India. It has survived from the third and second millennia B.C., from the period of the ancient Indus Valley civilization. Seals dating from this period depict the erect phallus with great frequency, and especially in conjunction with a horned deity, seated in a yogic pose, believed to be a prototype of Shiva. Shiva's flowing locks and the horns of the ancient deity represent the vital sexual energy that has accumulated and been transmuted into spiritual force.

Lingams are of various shapes, sizes, and materials. Perhaps the largest is the one that the Gods Brahma and Vishnu found one day when they were arguing, in the middle of limitless space, over who was the greatest God. Suddenly they saw a luminous pillar of flame that seemed to be without limit. So they decided to find it if had a beginning or end. Brahma went up and Vishnu flew down, but neither God could find the beginning or end of the flaming pillar. At that point Shiva appeared in the flames, saying that this pillar was his *lingam*, or phallus. Thereupon, Brahma and Vishnu realized that Shiva is the greatest God. This story is more popular among worshipers of Shiva than those of Brahma or Vishnu. Some worshipers simply fashion a *lingam* from sand on the seashore the way a child might construct a sandcastle. A dead tree stump, the base of an old, broken pillar, or a pillar of ice may equally serve as an object of worship. Each household generally has a *lingam* made according to scriptural formula and worshiped in the prescribed manner with offerings of incense, flowers, rice, lights, butter, and milk. In some sects the ritual premarital defloration of brides takes place with a Shiva *lingam*. The woman simply squats on the stone so that it penetrates her. Thus her first sexual encounter is with a God and serves as a model for the joy it is hoped she will share with her husband.

The Goddess is also worshiped in India. She is the creative field of feminine energy within every particle of existence. She straddles her lover Shiva in passionate abandon, moving in blissful waves that are the forms of creation. Worshipers of this pair perform long acts of ritual intercourse. First, they prepare themselves mentally and physically by practicing meditation and yoga postures, for it is only when the sensitivity of the organism has been deeply refined that the ultimate surrender becomes possible.

The purpose of the ritual is never orgasm in the ordinary sense, but an inner abandon in which both sexes realize their own spirituality. Thus the entire sexual act is used as a means of transcending ordinary sex. This ritual intercourse is called Tantra. Sexual energy which would otherwise be discharged downward and outward through focused genital tension and orgasm instead is drawn inward and upward, where it is transmuted into spiritual energy. In Indian eroticism, the sexual act and its fluids are always related to an underlying emotional field. The aim of Tantra is to use the sexual embrace to surrender to the most subtle and powerful spiritual force in the universe. The sexual fluids will flow according to the laws of the emotional field to which they are exposed. While lust will cause them to flow downward, spiritual love channels the energies of these substances upward, like the sap of a tree in spring, illuminating the heart and soul.

Tantra awakens increasing subtle and powerful energy fields within the body. These are experienced as a subtle body within the human body, much like the electromagnetism of the sun and earth. This subtle body has numerous channels through which rivers of energy course continually. The most important channel, called Rich in Happiness, runs like a gleaming thread from the base of the spine to the crown of the head. Along this channel are seven energy-transforming centers commonly represented in Indian art as lotuses. The lotus at the base of the spine has only four petals, while the one at the top of the head, signifying fully unfolded spirituality, has a thousand. In the lowest lotus at the base of the spine resides the coiled female energy, beautiful as a chain of lightning, known as Kundalini. Divinely quiescent, she is coiled around herself three times and slumbers, holding her tail in her mouth. As this dormant energy awakens, it rises, passing through each lotus, which lifts its drooping head and blooms. Since these so-called lotuses are energy transformers, as the Kundalini passes through each one, this activates increasingly powerful energy fields, drawing the sexual-spiritual energy higher and higher. This inner anatomy is the same in male and female. And according to this belief, anatomy is indeed destiny. The more one feels the subtle physiology of one's inner anatomy the more fulfilling life is. Thus those who unfold the lotus path transcend normal sexual distinctions and become psychologically androgynous.

Tantra uses several methods to arouse the Kundalini, including yoga postures, breathing exercises, meditation, and sexual union. In the Lotus Posture, one sits cross-legged, with each foot resting on the opposite thigh. This posture is considered the best for breathing exercises and meditation. Deep, rhythmic breathing harmonizes the functioning of the autonomic nervous system and charges the subtle body with energy. Another yoga exercise used to activate the Kundalini is called the Mulabanda. This exercise is performed by contracting the sphincter muscles of the rectum in conjunction with rhythmic breathing, and is similar to the Taoist deer exercise described in the preceding chapter.

The most powerful method of arousing the Kundalini is the sexual embrace. This embrace creates an energy field that raises sexual energy to its most exalted state. In order to help create this field, every minute detail of the ritual is carefully attended to. Both partners must be well rested. Furthermore, they must have mastered preliminary yoga, breathing, and meditation practices. It is important that the ritual be performed in a solitary place, free from intrusions, and at a propitious time, especially when there is a full moon. The preferred female partner is usually a young virgin, as virgins are thought to be full of spiritual power and capable of initiating one into the flow of subtle energies.

The first step in the ritual is bathing. Then the female is anointed with fragrant oils. Next, the couple sits cross-legged, facing one another and surrounded by flowers, burning incense, an oil lamp, and dishes of wine, meat, fish, and parched grain. These are then consumed. Each of these edibles is forbidden in orthodox Hinduism, so eating them in this ritual takes on some of the illicit allure that a first cigarette has for a Western teenager.

The man then touches each part of his partner's body while intoning the name of the Goddess. In this way, his partner loses her individuality and is ritually transformed into the Goddess. Then the male worships her by touching her right toe, legs, thighs, vulva, navel, heart, breasts, lips, forehead, then down the left side of her body in reverse order. Then he worships her vagina with incantations and offerings of flowers and sandalwood paste.

Next, he visualizes the Goddess and the God Shiva in sexual union, surrounded by a nimbus of light. He makes an offering of flowers. Then he worships his penis with flowers and incantations while breathing rhythmically. The woman holds her hands above his head, commanding him to immerse himself in her fully. They embrace, each sitting in the Lotus Posture, the woman on the man's lap and her legs around his waist. They sit motionless, allowing their energy to rise as they fall deeper and deeper into a limitless ocean of peace. In this embrace, genital orgasm is transcended, and the energy that would otherwise be discharged permeates the entire being.

This is certainly not romantic love, in which the lovers admire one another for their unique characteristics. Here the female is appreciated not as a woman but as the Goddess, and it doesn't matter greatly if she is one's wife or a total stranger as long as the union succeeds on the spiritual level. The strategy behind this form of embrace is to recoil from relationship with the gross physical world, the world of death and suffering, in favor of architectonic perfection of the subtle physiology. However suprapersonal Tantric union may seem, it has little in common with impersonal Taoist sexuality in which the woman is visualized not as the Goddess but as an enemy. Whereas Taoist sexuality in its manipulative forms depends upon active intercourse and control of the sexual energy, Tantric union does not. Rather, it is a contemplative, motionless surrender in which the sexual energy is allowed to move of its own accord without the interference of the will and gross physical stimulation. In this embrace increasingly subtle fields of energy unfold their soft textures and the union may thus deepen and expand for hours. The male retains his semen without much overt control, and both partners are left in a state of deep repose and fulfillment. Their subtle bodies merge in a single unified field.

Real lotuses bloom during the day. Conventional intercourse is like the blazing light of the sun, during which lotuslike women open physically to their lovers. Tantric union, however, is more like a spring night during which the so-called lotuses within the subtle body bloom like so many cowherd girls surrendering to the caresses of their Dark Lord; waves of sweetness wash the being, the dark shores of the soul are phosphorescent with them.

Fields

*P*HYSICS INFORMS US that material bodies are often surrounded by invisible energy forces called fields. Massive bodies like planets and stars have subtler bodies, their gravitational fields, that extend outward from them to infinity. The behavior of massive objects in space, as they orbit around other objects, is actually determined by these invisible gravitational fields.

The magnetic field of a compass plugs in to the magnetic field of the earth, allowing navigators to find their way even in cloudy weather. As we have seen, certain circles in ancient China and India used the vital, emotional, and spiritual fields within the human body to orient human love toward evolution and inner fulfillment.

Physics also informs us that electromagnetic energy is one of the four basic forces in the universe, binding together the electrons and protons of atoms in a ceaseless dance. Recent research in the West has discovered that there are bioelectrical currents streaming continuously through the human body, producing a total-body bioelectrical field that actually extends to infinity and thus is plugged in to the electromagnetic fields of the earth, the moon, and the farthest galaxies. This bioelectrical field, however, is little understood by Western science. Serious study began only in the 1970s. However, for thousands of years, Chinese and Indian cultures conceived of and experienced energy fields that pervaded the entire human organism. In fact, it can be said without exaggeration that their entire cultures are based on intimacy with these fields.

Long ago the Chinese realized that various organs in the physical body have corresponding energy fields. These energy fields are interwoven to form an integrated whole that is responsible for the harmonious functioning of the entire organism. The fields of energy can be influenced by stimulating points along a series of pathways called meridians, through which flows the energy the Chinese called *ch'i*.

In a healthy body *ch'i* circulates endlessly. Illness results from any obstruction in the flow. This causes an excess of energy in some organs and a deficiency in others. *Ch'i* is naturally strongest in various meridians during specific hours of the day and specific seasons. There have been many attempts to explain the nature of this energy, and recent research has shown that the meridians have a different electrical potential than the surrounding tissue.

The Chinese are very sensitive to fluctuations in the flow of *ch'i*. An abundance of *ch'i* gives one clear eyes, an audacious, powerful glance, sparkle, and agility. Just as a moving electrical current produces an electromagnetic field, the flow of *ch'i* creates a current of personal magnetism and vitality. When the *ch'i* is in harmony, the voice is soft and clear. A harsh voice shows a disharmonious *ch'i* or an excess of energy. A weak voice indicates a lack of *ch'i*. A rosy complexion, free of blemishes, is a sign of good *ch'i*. In the winter *ch'i* is concentrated in the organs and the core of the body; in the summer it is more prevalent in the head and surfaces of the skin. Atmospheric pressure and thunderstorms also affect the *ch'i*, as do sunny and cloudy weather and the emotions.

All the arts and sciences in ancient China dealt with the flow of *ch'i*, including medicine, massage, the martial arts, meditation, breathing exercises, and dance. Even painting, singing, writing poetry, cooking, or menial tasks such as butchering a hog require the circulation and expenditure of *ch'i*. Thus it is very difficult to separate these arts and sciences from each other and from ordinary life.

The martial arts provide a good example. From as early as the T'ang and Sung periods, there have been two schools of unarmed combat in China—the northern, exoteric tradition and the southern, esoteric tradition. The northern school was Buddhist, while the southern, or Wu-tang, tradition was Taoist and thus softer, based as it was on the principle of yielding. Anyone who has seen a karate demonstration will know that it is an aggressive art. Because of its emphasis on unrelenting attack and its use of kicking and hitting, karate is known as a "hard" form of combat, and is based on the northern or Buddhist school. Judo, which involves no hitting or kicking but yields to the force of the attacker in order to throw him or her off-balance, is a "soft" form based on the southern or Taoist school. *Tai chi chuan,* or "shadow boxing," is very popular in contemporary China, and it also is a product of the southern school. This martial art was developed long ago in a remote mountain complex of temples named Wu-tang shan. In modern China at dawn, when the *ch'i* in the atmosphere is most potent, many Chinese go to the parks in order to dance through the slow, graceful series of movements. *Tai chi* is also an ancient form of meditation, calming the mind. It is a breathing exercise, too, requiring deep, relaxed inhalation and exhalation. Yet it is a form of preventive medicine, because the *ch'i* is circulated through the meridians during the practice of *tai chi*. Moreover it has all the grace and beauty of a dance form. Yet it is a means of self-defense, a martial art. Thus a martial-arts expert, a temple dancer, an acupuncturist, a sexual alchemist, and a solitary sage will be working with the same energy of *ch'i*, learning to circulate it throughout the system of meridians, and then applying it to entertain, heal, make love, meditate, or defend. A specific point on a meridian may be attacked by a martial-arts expert, caressed by a lover, or massaged by a healer; all know that this point is a vital doorway into the vast inner fields that control the organism.

Modern Western biologists are aware that many biological functions take place according to daily rhythms. Doctors, for instance, know that every organ has its own cycle. A diseased organ will be worse at certain times of the day. Victims of Parkinson's disease may be completely free of symptoms in the evening, while asthma attacks are usually nocturnal. Fevers and body temperatures rise in the evening. Such examples could be multiplied many times. Thousands of years ago , however, the Chinese knew that people suffering from liver disease show no symptoms in the morning, experience increasing distress in the afternoon, and finally quiet down toward midnight. This, they said, is because the *ch'i* is stronger in specific organs and their meridians at different times. They knew that the energy fields of the organism acted as biological clocks sensitive to minute fluctuations in the energy field of the planet.

Whereas the emphasis in Western medicine is on treating the symptoms of an illness after it arises, Chinese medicine seeks to prevent disease by getting the body in touch with its inner fields of energy. When this energy is strong and fluid, no disease will stand much of a chance. Dealing with the subtle energy fields to prevent illness is much like the Taoist art of yielding in the martial arts. Rather than attacking the enemy directly, one cultivates an internal field of strength so that no enemy will attack. However, the maximum value of yielding, as in sexual practices, is to surrender to the softest thing in the universe, the Tao. As an ancient Chinese medicinal treatise advises, "The Yin and the Yang are contained within the Tao, the basic principle of the entire universe. They create all matter and its transmutations. The Tao is the beginning and the end; life and death; and it is found within the temples of the Gods. If you wish to cure disease, you must find this basic cause." By attuning one's spirit to the Tao, one puts all the meridians into balance. When disease does strike, the therapeutic range of acupuncture is great—but the emphasis is always on restoring strength and vitality to the entire body so that there will be no chance for disease to enter. Thus Chinese doctors were paid only as long as their patients remained well. The need to insert a needle into a patient was a sign that he or she was already seriously distant from the Tao.

Yet immortality, not mere physical health, was the ultimate Taoist concern. They believed that the subtle physiology, what the West might call the electric body, was capable of evolving. The energy could be circulated through the meridians via *tai chi,* massage, deep breathing, acupuncture, and sex. But that was only the beginning. The inner circulation of energy in a healthy body provided the basis for spiritual growth. The sexual energy was directed up the spine into the brain through meditation, directed down the front of the body, and then up the spine again. This inner circulation was more subtle than in the other meridians. Finally, the inner body of the practitioner would exit the physical body through the top of the head. Sexual techniques as well as solitary meditation were used to achieve this goal. The subtle physiology and its use in sex were a sort of ladder of spiritual achievement. In the art of dual cultivation, both the man and the woman meditate, then enter a motionless sexual embrace. With practice this was believed to cause the energy within their bodies to become "transcendental" and lead to a healthy long life and even immortality.

Indian culture is also very concerned with the subtle physiology. It is described as a series of 72,000 channels (*nadis*) through which flows an energy called *prana,* which is the same as the Chinese *ch'i.* Like *ch'i, prana* is most abundant in the early morning air and in the sexual fluids. Through correct breathing and sexual-yogic techniques, this energy circulates throughout the body, ensuring health and longevity. Like the Chinese, the Indians feel that the direction of human evolution is inward, through the subtle physiology. They, too, experience a channel of energy running the length of the spine to the brain where energy is transmuted into spiritual awareness. In India experiencing the subjective, spiritual world is the goal of life. Sex and the subtle physiology are a ladder to attain that goal. An Indian mystic who has written extensively on the experience of the subtle body is Gopi Krishna. In the account that follows he describes this awakening in classical Indian terms:

"One morning during the Christmas of 1937 I sat cross-legged in a small room in a little house on the outskirts of the town of Jammu, the winter capital of the Jammu and Kashmir State in northern India. I was meditating with my face towards the window on the east through which the first grey streaks of the slowly brightening dawn fell into the room. Long practice had accustomed me to sit in the same posture for hours at a time without the least discomfort, and I sat breathing slowly and rhythmically, my attention drawn toward the crown of my head, contemplating an imaginary lotus in full bloom, radiating light.

"I sat steadily, unmoving and erect, my thoughts uninterruptedly centered on the shining lotus, intent on keeping my attention from wandering and bringing it back again and again whenever it moved in any other direction. The intensity of concentration interrupted my breathing; gradually it slowed down to such an extent that at times it was barely perceptible. My whole being was so engrossed in the contemplation of the lotus that for several minutes at a time I lost touch with my body and surroundings.

"During such intervals I used to feel as if I were poised in mid-air, without any feeling of a body around me. The only object of which I was aware was a lotus of brilliant colour, emitting rays of light. This experience has happened to many people who practise meditation in any form regularly for a sufficient length of time, but what followed on that fateful morning in my case, changing the whole course of my life and outlook, has happened to few.

"During one such spell of intense concentration I

suddenly felt a strange sensation below the base of my spine, at the place touching the seat, while I sat cross-legged on a folded blanket spread on the floor. The sensation was so extraordinary and so pleasing that my attention was forcibly drawn towards it.

"The moment my attention was thus unexpectedly withdrawn from the point on which it was focused, the sensation ceased. Thinking it to be a trick played by my imagination to relax the tension, I dismissed the matter from my mind and brought my attention back to the point from which it had wandered. Again I fixed it on the lotus, and as the image grew clear and distinct at the top of my head, again the sensation occurred.

"This time I tried to maintain the fixity of my attention and succeeded for a few seconds, but the sensation extending upwards grew so intense and was so extraordinary, as compared to anything I had experienced before, that in spite of myself my mind went towards it, and at that very moment it again disappeared. I was now convinced that something unusual had happened for which my daily practice of concentration was probably responsible.

"I had read glowing accounts, written by learned men, of great benefits resulting from concentration, and of the miraculous powers acquired by yogis through such exercises. My heart began to beat wildly, and I found it difficult to bring my attention to the required degree of fixity. After a while I grew composed and was soon as deep in meditation as before. When completely immersed I again experienced the sensation, but this time, instead of allowing my mind to leave the point where I had fixed it, I maintained a rigidity of attention throughout.

"The sensation again extended upwards, growing

in intensity, and I felt myself wavering; but with a great effort I kept my attention centered on the lotus. Suddenly, with a roar like that of a waterfall, I felt a stream of liquid light entering my brain through the spinal cord.

"Entirely unprepared for such a development, I was completely taken by surprise; but regaining self-control instantaneously, I remained sitting in the same posture, keeping my mind on the point of concentration. The illumination grew brighter and brighter, the roaring louder, I experienced a rocking sensation and then felt myself slipping out of my body, entirely enveloped in a halo of light.

"It is impossible to describe the experience accurately. I felt the point of consciousness that was myself growing wider, surrounded by waves of light. It grew wider and wider, spreading outward while the body, normally the immediate object of its perception, appeared to have receded into the distance until I became entirely unconscious of it.

"I was now all consciousness, without any outline, without any idea of a corporeal appendage, without any feeling or sensation coming from the senses, immersed in a sea of light simultaneously conscious and aware of every point, spread out, as it were, in all directions without any barrier or material obstruction. I was no longer myself, or to be more accurate, no longer as I knew myself to be, a small point of awareness confined in a body, but instead was a vast circle of consciousness in which the body was but a point, bathed in light and in a state of exaltation and happiness impossible to describe.

"After some time, the duration of which I could not judge, the circle began to narrow down; I felt myself contracting, becoming smaller and smaller, until I again became dimly conscious of my body, then more clearly; and as I slipped back to my old condition, I became suddenly aware of the noises in the street, felt again my arms and legs and head, and once more became my narrow self in touch with my body and surroundings."[9]

Only a few years ago such an experience would have been considered bizarre in the West. Recently, however, millions of Westerners have been practicing meditation and contemplation, with the result that such experiences are becoming much more frequent. Western science, however, is only beginning to understand bioelectrical fields in the human body, and it is practically ignorant of the more subtle emotional and spiritual fields with which they interweave. Unlike their Eastern counterparts, who tend to look at the body from a subjective, inside-out approach, Western scientists study the body from the outside. In Western medicine a battle has been waged for the past few hundred years between chemical and electrical concepts of the body. Like the Chinese and Indians, early Western scientists from the time of the Greeks thought that the body must be animated by some vital force. Many believed that this must be electricity, but in 1868 a German scientist, Julius Bernstein, theorized that nerve impulses were basically chemical interactions. This news came at about the same time that Pasteur showed that infectious diseases are caused by bacteria and that Claude Bernard demonstrated the biochemical basis of digestion and energy utilization. The chemical basis of life was becoming firmly established.

However, by 1900 electricity was making quite a name for itself in the physical sciences. Telephones, light bulbs, and radios were soon to become common household items. Electromagnetic energy began to be generated, transmitted, received, and converted in an increasing number of ways, and the electromagnetic environment became polluted overnight. Yet scientists, backed by growing energy companies and pharmaceutical industries, still denied that electricity played any role whatever in living organisms. A few experiments, however, were performed. When a human head was placed in a strong magnetic field, it produced a subjective experience of light. Narcosis was caused in animals by passing an alternating current through their heads. Electroshock therapy for schizophrenia was discovered. And the electroencephalogram was developed to measure electrical waves in the brain. But then in the 1920s scientists proved Bernstein's theory that the transmission between nerves was chemical. Electricity, it seemed, had no significant place in biology. After all, if the biochemistry of an organism could be made healthy by attending to a more subtle and pervasive bioelectrical field, where would this leave the growing pharmaceutical industry?

Only very recently has serious research been undertaken in the West to investigate the relationship between electromagnetism and life, and what has been found is very exciting. According to Robert Becker, an American scientist whose recent book, *The Body Electric*, documents the latest findings in bioelectrical research, there are electrical currents that flow continually throughout the human body. Although these currents differ from previously known electrical currents in the nervous system, they seem to provide very general information to the nervous system. Because the currents pervade the entire body, like the meridians of the Chinese and the Indian *nadis*, they produce a coherent, total-body field that is detectable with instruments. Some scientists now think that this field may integrate thousands of biological systems within the body into a unified whole.

This discovery of an electromagnetic body will have profound consequences in the biological sciences, changing the way we think about the environment, medicine, and sex. An important question presently being investigated is how our electromagnetic body interacts with other electromagnetic fields in the environment, both natural and artificial. The Chinese gave a great deal of attention to the influence of environmental forces on *ch'i*. They advised that making love or performing acupuncture during electrical storms would disturb the flow of *ch'i*, making it "jumpy." In the West we know that the earth has a magnetic field. Recently it has been discovered that this field is subject to variations ranging from daily fluctuations to dramatic changes taking place over thousands of years, during which the North and South poles reverse. The earth's electromagnetic field is also sensitive to the electromagnetic fields of the sun, the moon, and the galaxy. The space between the surface of the earth and the surrounding ionosphere forms a cavity like a huge echo chamber. Here electromagnetic waves resonate in micropulsations ranging from 0.01 to 20 cycles per second. Lightning emits electromagnetic waves of all frequencies, but only those that are within the spectrum of the earth's ionospheric cavity survive, resonating back and forth between the Northern and Southern hemispheres before dying out.

A recent theory proposes that at the time life was forming on earth, our planet's ionospheric cavity generated powerful electromagnetic currents in the atmosphere. These resonated at a frequency of ten cycles per second. Therefore, this resonant frequency may have been imprinted on the first living molecules. This may explain why this frequency is common to many animals, including humans. In fact, this waveband is especially prominent during meditation.

Many biological cycles are affected by natural electromagnetic forces. Birds, bees, and many other animals navigate using the earth's electromagnetic field as a compass. It is known that oysters open their shells at high tide to feed. But how do they know to do so? Do they feel the water splashing against them and then open? If you remove oysters from the ocean and put them in water in a laboratory with constant light and temperature, they continue to open their shells in synchrony with the tides. Furthermore, if the oysters are flown inland, thousands of miles from the ocean, they continue to open in synchrony with the tides of their original home. However, over a period of a few weeks they will gradually change— opening as if there were an ocean and tides in their new inland home. Thus they are capable of reading variations in the earth's electromagnetic field caused by the lunar tidal pattern. Many other species, including humans, have biological cycles linked with rhythms in the earth's normal electromagnetic field. Such diverse phenomena as oxygen consumption in potatoes and lymphocyte levels in the human bloodstream are triggered by fluctuations in this field.

What happens, however, when humans are removed from their natural electromagnetic environment? One experiment placed a group of people in a completely dark room, where their biological clocks could not tune in to cycles of light and dark. Another group was placed in a completely dark room that was also shielded from all electromagnetic fields. Various daily biological cycles were then measured, including body temperature, sleep, and metabolism. The cycles of those who were not shielded from the natural electromagnetic environment maintained essentially normal rates, even though the subjects had no idea of telling time by the daily alternation of light and dark. The electromagnetic fields in their bodies somehow knew and informed the rest of the organism.

However, those subjects who were in the room shielded from natural electromagnetic fields soon became totally unsynchronized, their biological rhythms losing any relationship to the normal daily rhythms. When an artificial electrical field of ten cycles per second was introduced into this room, the subjects' biological rhythms began to return to normal. In other words, the body's electromagnetic field acts as an antenna, tuning in to the electromagnetic field of the earth, which in turn responds to the electromagnetic fields of the sun, the moon, and the galaxy. It is important to remember that the ten-cycles-per-second frequency is found in the brain waves of all the higher mammals and is especially prominent during meditation.

Minute fluctuations in the earth's electromagnetic field serve as a kind of clock responsible for cueing thousands of biological cycles in the body, including those of metabolism, growth, and reproduction. Yet electromagnetic "smog" is the most polluted aspect of our environment. From the time of the origin of life on earth to the beginning of the twentieth century, the only electromagnetic forces on earth were natural ones. However, by the 1950s, artificial electromagnetic fields became more dominant than natural fields. Except in isolated forests it is difficult to find an environment in the United States in which artificial electric and magnetic background levels are not very high. In the vicinity of such artificial sources as television and radio broadcasting stations, walkie-talkies, microwave relay antennas, household appliances like television sets, computers, electric blankets, broilers, lamps, etc., the levels are much higher. We are also subjected to radiant energy from communications satellites. Our daily exposure to electromagnetic fields is two hundred million times greater than that of our pre-twentieth-century ancestors. We have half a million miles of high-power lines in the United States. There are nine million broadcasting transmitters and relay stations, thirty million CB radios, 250,000 microwave telecommunications links, 125 million television sets; eight million microwave ovens, well over ten million computers, and numerous major military sources such as radar, missile-guidance systems, and communications equipment. We have electronic games, electric garage-door openers, and countless other sources of electromagnetic pollution.

The Soviet Union has been conducting research on the bioeffects of electromagnetism since the 1930s. Until 1982, allowable exposure levels in the United States were ten thousand times higher than in the Soviet Union. Now our legal exposure levels are only a thousand times as high. The danger this represents to our health is significant. Consider that in Moscow the United States Embassy was flooded with microwave signals for fourteen years. During this time, those living in the embassy had white-blood-cell counts that were 40 percent higher than normal. Three children had to return to the United States to be treated for blood disorders. One ambassador had to resign his post because of a rare blood disease and bleeding from the eyes. Both his predecessors died of cancer. Sixteen women residents developed breast cancer. Yet the emissions from a typical American microwave oven are higher than the highest exposures at the embassy in Moscow.

In such an environment, how is an organism to discriminate among the vast array of electromagnetic signals? Is it not possible, especially in cities where there are great concentrations of electromagnetic "smog," that exposure could confuse the integrated functioning of the electromagnetic body, which depends upon clear electromagnetic signals from the natural environment to synchronize thousands of biological processes? It has been found that suicides and childhood cancer are more prevalent among those who live near high-power lines. Other studies have shown that artificial electromagnetic fields have definite effects on the cardiovascular system. People who work around radar, radio transmitters, television terminals, and various kinds of industrial equipment may be subject to abnormal changes in their cardiovascular, endocrine, hemotological, and nervous systems. This electromagnetic bombardment cannot always be solved by moving to the country. Even in Oregon, residents suffer from the pollution of an electromagnetic signal aimed at them from the most powerful radio transmitter in the world, located in Kiev, deep in the Soviet Union. It would be naïve to think that the United States is not also doing research on electromagnetic warfare.

While many artificial sources of electromagnetic radiation can confuse the body's sensitivity to the natural fields it relies on, not all natural fields produce positive effects on life. For instance, electromagnetic storms on the sun may trigger psychotic episodes in humans and lower immune-system strength. It must be added, however, that not *all* artificial fields are detrimental. In fact, special ones are used to heal bone fractures that otherwise would not heal. However, the most effective way to ensure the electromagnetic integrity of the body is through meditation, which plugs in to the ten-cycles-per-second resonant frequency believed to have been present at the formation of life on earth. (This may explain why ten cycles per second is the primary frequency in all animals and why they exhibit such extreme sensitivity to it.) Meditation can normalize circadian rhythms in humans shielded from the natural electromagnetic signals of the earth, moon, and sun. Meditation provides the system with a means of maintaining electromagnetic integrity that is relatively immune to disruption by artificial and adverse natural radiation.

But how are living things affected by the electromagnetic fields of other creatures? All animals produce brain waves of 10 cycles per second, and under certain conditions these waves *may* serve as a kind of interspecies communications link. Some of the most advanced brain-wave research is being carried out at Maharishi International University in Fairfield, Iowa. At the university researchers have found that increasingly enlightened and creative levels of consciousness are characterized by increased brain-wave coherence. In fact, the orderly brain waves of groups of subjects meditating together seems to affect the brain-wave coherence of the surrounding nonmeditating populations, resulting in dramatic decreases in illness, crime, and accidents. Such research is very much in its infancy, but it clearly indicates that there are intelligent and powerful alternatives to the electromagnetic warfare being researched by national defense departments.

The Taoist art of defense relies on the activation of subtle fields. Modern guerrilla warfare is based on influencing "the hearts and minds" of the people, thereby creating a strong psychological basis of support for guerrilla activities. Those who practice meditation, especially in groups, are not only protecting themselves from electromagnetic pollution, but through their brain waves are actually enlivening a field of peace, creativity, and orderliness that influences the hearts and minds of others in a positive and subtle manner. The ancient Taoist sages would agree that military conflicts are possible only in an area in which this subtle field is not enlivened through meditation.

If two or more people were to meditate in close physical proximity, they would be able to generate a powerful electromagnetic field that would mutually uplift and purify them, forming an electromagnetic antenna to tune in to natural electromagnetic currents from terrestial and cosmic sources. If a man and woman approach physical intimacy in a contemplative, meditative way, they can generate the same brain-wave frequencies as those produced in solitary meditation. However, the electromagnetic field they produce would be much stronger than if they were isolated from each other. There are probably deeper, more subtle energy fields not yet discovered by science which such a couple would enjoy.

Thus recent scientific findings support the Chinese and Indian experiences that there is a power or force within a man and a woman that is contacted during sexual union, and that by surrendering to this energy one can gain health and spiritual illumination. However, these recent findings by biologists have not yet been integrated into Western sexology. The widest gulf separating the Western mind from more mature traditions is the former's incapacity to understand the sacred value of sex—and thus embodied life—to live sexual life as a sacrament. In more traditional cultures sex is a sacrament, an occasion to commune with the very essence and mystery of life. Taoists and Tantrics have always insisted that their sexual embraces are radically different from profane sexual intercourse. But their rituals are too little understood, too complex and esoteric, to be adopted readily by modern lovers. There are numerous books on Tantra, for instance, which only hint at the subject of sexuality, dwelling instead on arcane philosophical matters. The ancient tradition from which Tantra evolved has become encrusted with weighty religious and philosophical concerns that obscure its vitality. And though there are some Tantric gurus in the United States and Europe, their teachings are heavily shrouded in Hindu theology that too often leaves their followers concerned more with beads and incense than with lovemaking. One can enter the core of spiritual sexuality neither by Hinduizing one's own approach to sex nor by Westernizing a Hindu or Taoist approach.

If a genuine sexual-spiritual union is to unfold on Western soil it must be discovered spontaneously and grow innocently within its universal source—the embrace of lovers. And while we may learn from other, more ancient experiments, we must not be tempted to imitate them, for in doing so there is a danger of ending up with only the outer trappings.

Fortunately, there has been some Western exploration in this area. In the mid-nineteenth century the art of sexual-spiritual union was discovered by an

American, John Noyes, who later popularized the technique. He called it "karezza" (pronounced kar-ET-za), from the Italian *carezza*, or "caress." Couples who practiced the technique began to have profound spiritual experiences such as holy love for one another (after years of boredom), feelings of immense joy, luminosity, and rapture lasting for many hours, following prolonged periods of lovemaking. Several books were published on karezza, hundreds of couples experienced it, but Victorian prudery was sufficient to prevent the practice from gaining a lasting foothold. Finally, it was all but forgotten.

The manner in which karezza was discovered in America speaks well for the importance of attitude in sexuality, for, in sharp contrast to the ancient Chinese attitude toward women, it came about as a result of a man's deep and abiding concern for his wife. In 1838, John Noyes married a beautiful woman and experienced the usual sexual life until 1846. It was during this eight-year period that he studied the subject of sexual intercourse and discovered the principle of karezza. The discovery itself was forced upon him by sorrowful experiences. In the course of six years, his wife went through five births. Four of them were premature: only one child lived. This experience directed and helped him continue his studies of sexuality. After their last disappointment, he promised his wife never again to expose her to such suffering. He had made up his mind to live separately from her rather than break his promise.

This was his situation in the summer of 1844. He began to reason that the sexual organs have a social function that is quite distinct from the generative function, and that these two functions may be separated beneficially and practically. Noyes experimented with this concept and found it greatly increased his and his wife's sexual enjoyment. He communicated his discovery to a friend. The friend's experience was the same. In the course of the next two years, Noyes studied his new theory more thoroughly and published a pamphlet on it. Later he founded a community that practiced this method of intercourse, and he studied those results carefully. Without exception he found that karezza, if properly practiced, is of genuine benefit to all aspects of life.

Noyes's theory is as follows: There is a magnetic force in humans that is exchanged during sexual intercourse. This force he called "social magnetism." Noyes stated furthermore that the male sexual organs are generally understood to have two distinct functions—the urinary and the reproductive. But he argued that there are really *three* functions—the urinary, the reproductive, and the loving—i.e., these organs are conductors of social magnetism. The loving function is as distinct from the reproductive function as the reproductive is from the urinary. In fact, strictly speaking, the generative organs are physiologically distinct from the organs of union in both male and female. The testicles, the male's generative organs, and the female uterus are separate from the organs of union. The sexual union of male and female no more requires the emission of semen than of urine. For Noyes the purpose of sexual intercourse is the interchange of magnetic influences through the motionless union of the sexual organs. This last point is very important. Discharge of the semen and the pleasure that accompanies it can be brought about by masturbation, and is not necessarily a dual affair but a personal one. The exchange of magnetic influence, however, is essentially a social process. In fact, Noyes claimed that karezza vastly increases the pleasure of sexual intercourse.

Following the publication of Noyes's ideas, Alice Bunker Stockham, one of the first female doctors in the United States, began to do her own research on the technique, which she published in her book *Karezza: Ethics of Marriage*. In the quaint language of her era she describes the technique briefly:

> At the appointed time, without fatigue of body or unrest of mind, accompany general bodily contact with expressions of endearment and affection, followed by the complete but quiet union of sexual organs. During a lengthly period of perfect control, the whole being is merged into the other, and an exquisite exaltation experienced. In the course of an hour the physical tension subsides, the spiritual exaltation increases, and not uncommonly, visions of a transcendent life are seen and consciousness of new powers experienced.[10]

It was not until early in the twentieth century, however, that an American physician, Dr. Friedrich Von Urban, began to do serious research on karezza. His studies continued for more than thirty years. He was reluctant to publish his findings because he could not prove them scientifically, even though he found karezza worked perfectly well in everyday life. When he did publish finally, he used the terms "electricity" and "electrical streams" to describe the exchange of energies during karezza. Yet he cautiously stated that the relationship of electricity to biological matters was somewhat beyond the realm of the science of his day. His terminology would have been well supported by current research showing the influence of electromagnetism on life, especially the discovery of a whole-body electromagnetic field.

Von Urban taught that even when a man and woman are happily married, the bliss does not last for long. Often marriages end in disaster. He found in his private practice that the most frequent reason for marriages to bog down in intolerance, anger, and hostility was a more or less unconscious resentment over sexual disappointment. The reason a couple love one another at first and then begin to grow apart is because the nature of sex is not properly understood.

Experience convinced Von Urban that there is a difference in bioelectrical potential between males and females that can be exchanged during intercourse, leaving both lovers relaxed and fulfilled. This theory was suggested to him by his knowledge of sex from four different areas:

1. The experiences of a Near Eastern couple
2. The knowledge of the sexual lives and taboos of certain tribal peoples, especially the Polynesians
3. His study of the followers of the karezza technique in the United States
4. Observations of a neurotic patient

The first experience concerns a couple in Damascus, Syria. The male was a former patient of Dr. Von Urban who related that he had married a very lovely young Arabian woman. They both loved each other very much. One night the man and his wife had been lying naked for about an hour on a couch, hugging and caressing each other but without engaging in sexual intercourse. The room was totally dark. When the couple separated from each other the wife became visible. An aura of greenish-blue light circled her entire body. The husband reached for her, but when his hand came within an inch of her, an electric spark sprang from her to himself. It was visible, audible, and painful.

Upon hearing the story, Von Urban was surprised. He thought secretly that the young man had perhaps been hallucinating. Then he remembered that the embryo is composed of three layers of cells: the endoderm (innermost layer), the source of the vital organs; the mesoderm (middle layer), which forms the muscles, bones, and sinews; and the ectoderm (outer layer), which forms the skin and nerves. The ancient Chinese, knowing that the skin and nerves are closely connected in the embryo, derived the system of acupuncture. From Western science Von Urban knew that the electrical impulses of the nervous system could possibly be transmitted through the skin, since the two types of tissue have the same origin in the ectoderm.

Von Urban persuaded the newly married couple to help him conduct some experiments. In the first, husband and wife, after lying naked and in close embrace for one hour in a dark room, had sexual intercourse lasting only five minutes. Both attained satisfaction. When they stood up again, however, the sparks began to jump between their bodies. This indicated that while the couple had been superficially gratified by orgasm, their bioelectrical potential had not been neutralized. Several days later, the couple again had intercourse. This time it lasted for fifteen minutes. Once more the sparks appeared.

A few days later the couple's intercourse lasted for twenty-seven minutes. Following this period no sparks were visible. Von Urban concluded that the twenty-seven-minute period was the determining factor. In another series of experiments on the same couple, the doctor learned that if they did not lie naked for at least a half-hour, preferably longer, in close, loving physical contact but instead began to have intercourse without any prior contact, no aura formed around the body of the woman, nor did the sparks appear. This was true even though the sexual union was less than the twenty-seven-minute duration thought necessary to eliminate these phenomena. In Indian Tantra, it is known that the flow of energy from one lover to the other begins to take place after thirty-two minutes of motionless intercourse. The husband and wife found that every episode of intercourse less than twenty-seven minutes long brought on in both of them an urgent desire to repeat the sexual union. However, if this desire was fulfilled by another too-brief consummation, both lovers became irritable and at times experienced headache, heart palpitations, asthma, and other symptoms. This indicated that although local tension in the sexual organs had been relieved through orgasm, the tension in the entire body and spirit had not. The bioelectrical potential had not been neutralized. Furthermore, intercourse of short duration increased the distance from which sparks leaped, showing that the tension in their bodies became stronger with each successive intercourse of less than twenty-seven minutes.

Intercourse that lasted a half-hour or more, however, was generally followed by total relaxation and no desire to repeat the act. In fact, the couple's desire for sex did not usually reappear for five or six days to a week. And their feelings of love for one another were very deep. They experienced the same feelings of relaxation and love, even after very brief periods of intercourse, if the husband did not withdraw his penis from his wife's vagina, but, rather, remained inside her for at least half an hour, even though his penis was not erect. During this period of time he would give his attention fully to the point of contact of their sexual organs.

The couple found that sexual union lasting for a half-hour gave them fulfillment that continued for five days, intercourse lasting an hour satisfied them both for about a week, and intercourse lasting two hours long brought fulfillment for two weeks. This same abiding relaxation was also brought about by prolonged bodily contact without normal sexual intercourse or even penetration. This is in agreement with John Noyes's theory that the loving or magnetic function of sex can be separated from the reproductive function.

Von Urban's experiments were corroborated further by his study of the sexual mores of certain tribal peoples. Some Polynesian societies, he observed, rub their infants with the palms of their hands for hours to keep them tranquil. It is a common practice for the mothers to carry their infants on the naked skin of their backs. While these mothers work, the babies are in close physical contact and remain happy and peaceful. Von Urban felt that this physical contact neutralized the bioelectrical potential in the infants, keeping them free of tension. He was also acquainted with the fact that babies who are not breast-fed are popularly believed by the Polynesians to be handicapped in their love life. Polynesian women, who caress their children for hours, seem to pass on instinctively an attitude toward love for which these people are famous. Havelock Ellis observed long ago that infant mortality is about 30 percent higher among children who are not exposed frequently to caressing and petting.

Polynesian methods of lovemaking also impressed Von Urban. The frequency of intercourse is usually not greater than once every five days. On all other nights, couples sleep together in close bodily contact, but avoid contact between sexual organs. When they do make love, foreplay and caressing last for at least an hour, during which time they kiss, embrace, and bite one another. After the man enters the woman's vagina, the couple lie united in a motionless embrace for at least a half-hour, often longer, before they begin moving and thrusting. After orgasm they continue to lie together, with sexual organs still united, for a lengthy period. Dr. Von Urban was delighted to learn of these sexual traditions, for they verified his theory that happy married life depends upon successfully awakening the "electrical streams" by foreplay, then allowing the currents to be equalized by prolonged contact.

The inhabitants of the Trobriand Islands in British New Guinea mock the sexual technique of white people. They amuse mixed audiences with caricatures of Western lovers. In the experience of these islanders, Westerners perform sex too hurriedly. Trobrianders believe that love should proceed slowly. They say that "after one hour the souls of the ancestors awaken and bless our union." The long duration of lovemaking is for them a sacred duty, a tradition that arose, no doubt, to appease human emotions as well as those of the spirits.

The position many South Sea Islanders assume in lovemaking is also instructive. The idea is to be completely free from any strain or pressure. The body should be entirely relaxed. Therefore, the man never lies on top of the woman. During the long sexual encounters of these people, such a position would be unthinkable. Even if the male were to ease his weight by supporting himself with his arms, he would not be relaxed.

On those nights when no sexual intercourse takes place, couples sleep together at opposite ends of a sleeping mat. Their two open pairs of legs fit together like two pairs of scissors. In this way the sexual organs come into closest possible contact without actual penetration of the vagina, thus allowing the tensions in the organs to subside.

On days of intercourse, all forms of lovemaking including kissing, biting, embracing, rubbing, etc., are considered essential. On other nights, however, no tender caresses are allowed. Although a couple may lie close together, body to body, naked, and find themselves deeply relaxed in the morning, they do not kiss or excite each other. By observing these rules, they create a love life that overflows into their daily living, and they are practically free of neuroses.

In studying the writings of John Noyes and Alice Stockman, Dr. Von Urban learned that karezza is characterized by prolonged, motionless union. In about a half-hour, a subjective but very real and delightful sensation begins to be felt, usually lasting as long as the embrace is maintained, which might be for several hours. The two partners may then simply fall into a deep, refreshing, dreamless sleep. The following day they experience a state of exaltation and relaxation that may last for days. Usually the couple feels a deepening love for each other and for the world about them.

A fourth, very instructive, source of information for Dr. Von Urban was the sex life of a neurotic woman with whom he was acquainted. In his description, she was an extremely beautiful woman of twenty-three years of age. Psychoanalysis had been useless in her case. Dr. Von Urban found a job for her in his sanitarium. Her main problem was her fear of men. From the time of puberty no man had ever been able even to touch her. She was the object of desire of many young men, but all failed in winning her affection. She had been raped by her stepfather when she was still a child.

Dr. Von Urban's assistant fell in love with her. After many months she consented to marry him under one condition, that he would never make any physical advances. After six weeks of marriage the couple spent their first night together in bed. They were both naked. They embraced, but the young man had to live up to his promise and not have sexual intercourse. They lay close together, and after about a half hour began to feel as if every cell of their bodies was alive with radiance and bliss. This produced a rapture such as neither had felt before. After some more time in this embrace they had the experience of merging into one. Time, body, and awareness of physical space began to dissolve. All thought ceased. They both described the experience as "superhuman," or "divine." They felt as if they had literally entered Heaven. This experience lasted throughout the entire night. Then a sense of suffocation set in. But if they got up and took a shower, they could go back to bed and reenter this state of bliss. The following day they were both happy and relaxed.

Learning from these experiences, Von Urban prescribed a sexual union for his patients that allowed a free and prolonged exchange of bioelectrical currents. As a result many couples who were seeking divorce were reconciled, and many physical disorders, such as high blood pressure, ulcers, and skin diseases, were cured. One patient, a man of about thirty, was underweight and suffering from stomach ulcers, high blood pressure, headaches, heart pain, and general nervousness. For two years he had felt so much anxiety that he was unable to work, sleep, read, write, or listen to music. He had even attempted suicide. When questioned by Von Urban, the man replied that his sex life was quite normal—he always practiced *coitus interruptus* and intercourse lasted only a couple of minutes. Von Urban, realizing that his bioelectrical energy was first being stimulated, then blocked, suggested he change his sex life so that these currents could flow within him and toward his wife. Following Von Urban's instructions, within two weeks the man became quiet and relaxed and gained twenty pounds. All his physical symptoms disappeared because he had normalized the bioelectrical field of his body by merging with that of his wife in prolonged intimate embrace.

From such experience Von Urban came to the following conclusions:

1. That lovers fully awake in each other's presence stimulate streams of bioelectrical energy within each other.
2. That these bioelectrical streams, once excited, require at least twenty-seven minutes of conductivity between two bodies to flow and merge into a unified field.
3. Once aroused by kissing and caressing, these streams flow through the lips, nipples, breasts, arms, and legs of the lovers, passing back and forth between them and bringing about a state of complete relaxation and fulfillment—even without penetration, intercourse, or conventional orgasm.
4. The bioelectrical streams have a tendency to

flow to the penis and vagina, and motionless union of these two sexual organs for at least twenty-seven minutes will allow these currents to merge.

5. Even in conventional, active intercourse, should the male ejaculate prematurely, if he does not withdraw his penis from the vagina but waits for at least twenty-seven minutes, the bioelectrical streams will merge, bringing full relaxation to both partners.

6. When the bioelectrical streams have unified into one energy field, no need for repetition of the sexual act will be felt for about five days.

7. Hurried intercourse, menstruation, and ovulation increase bioelectrical tension in the body. If not alleviated, this tension can disturb normal cellular processes, even produce disease.

8. Psychological factors such as love, fear, anger, and resentment interact with the bioelectrical forces. When love is felt, the streams flow freely; but negative, contracted emotions block the flow.

Like the Chinese and the Indians, Von Urban recognized that the flow of bioelectrical energy is important, and facilitating its flow can prevent or cure many physical and psychological ailments. He also recognized that emotions play an important part in the merging of bioelectrical energies.

Whether we look to the Taoist method of dual cultivation, to the Indian Tantric embrace, or to American experiences, we find that a man and a woman are like two halves of a battery. If they join together in a certain manner, they are capable of entering a much more powerful energy field than during conventional sex. When they surrender to this field, the couple can enjoy a prolonged whole-body orgasm that is quite different from localized genital orgasm. The boundaries between two bodies and souls simply disappear. Since this approach is based on surrender and receptivity to whole-body feeling, it may seem somewhat passive or "feminine." In fact, many of the women interviewed in *The Hite Report* desired this type of physical intimacy as much as or more than conventional intercourse, and wished that they could experience it more often. Yet it requires that *both* partners become receptive to deep, refined emotion and overwhelming energy fields. To open up to these levels of experience, men have much to learn from women, assuming, of course, that these women have not become habituated to the typical male pattern of conventional intercourse.

With respect to the unfolding of these deeply blooming energies, virginity is a great asset, for a virgin's vital energy has not yet become accustomed to being short-circuited and expressed through the genitals. When it is not dammed up, but finds an outlet in intense physical, intellectual, or emotional activities such as sports, academics, and religion, the sexual vitality of virginity is habituated, rather, to nourishing the entire body and its activities. Endowed with this innate, innocent functional disposition, virginal energies can flow easily and naturally into expressions of profound emotion and radiant whole-body pleasure when one is in an intimate embrace. It is also natural, alas, for innocence actively to seek its own loss, especially when it is bombarded with the propaganda of conventional and not-so-conventional (read "perverted") intercourse. Seeking to become "experienced," innocence gladly throws to the wind a disposition for which it may later yearn.

One difficulty with this "field" approach to physical intimacy, then, is that it requires a free-flowing
energy along with an ability to surrender to this force.
Many men, whether virginal or experienced, will feel
that this approach is too feminine to be considered.
After all, one of the most important ways men define
their masculinity is through sex, and many feel they
must perform actively, athletically stimulating their
partners to multiple orgasms. Making love is like
making an artifact or constructing a building—piling
up brick after brick, plateau after plateau, orgasm after
orgasm. For such men, emotional surrender is something women do. To yield quietly to swelling waves
of energy would be a threat to the whole bodily held
"masculine" emotional stance.

In Taoism, however, to yield is to embrace the superior power of the feminine, so much stronger than
the hard, controlled masculine. And many men would
do well to heed Lao Tzu's advice to "know the masculine, but keep to the feminine." Know the active,
but keep to the passive. For in receptivity we are capable of opening to radiant gardens of energy. Love
is not like a building that we make or construct, but
like a tree that grows, shaping itself from within and
according to the laws of its own being. This is the
meaning of the ascending series of lotuses that open
to Tantric lovers during their subtle embrace. The
down-turned, closed lotus buds swell with energy, turn
upward, and then, with a force that is just the opposite of grasping, they blossom.

This approach to love not only is opposed to the
macho self-image that disallows deep emotional and
physical surrender, displays an obsession with performance, and finds fulfillment in localized genital

excitation, but, as Dr. Von Urban discovered, any emotional immaturity between sexual partners tends to block the exchange of bioelectrical energies. Emotional and spiritual fields are interwoven with these vital energy fields and are mutually reinforcing.

Von Urban tells of a couple he saw in 1928 at a café on the Boulevard Clichy in Paris, a spot where local artists gathered. There was an exceptionally attractive couple seated near him. The dramatic nature of their relationship had become well known in the quarter. Rudolph was a penniless writer, and his girl friend, Mimi, lived with him. When Von Urban saw them in the café, they suddenly erupted into a violent argument. Mimi, shaken, left the café, screaming that this time she was not coming back. Rudolph hurled his drink after her, shouting that now, at last, he could concentrate on his writing.

Von Urban's professional interest was aroused. He engaged the young man in conversation. Rudolph soon confided that in the beginning their relationship had been very sweet. After a couple of months, however, Mimi became quarrelsome. They would argue. She would leave, only to return after a few days. Then they would make love passionately, very frequently, but for a very brief duration. Mimi would come to orgasm even before they had intercourse, so there was never a prolonged union.

Dr. Von Urban tried to convince Rudolph that the frequency of his orgasms was draining his energy and his capacity for writing. He also informed the young man that if intercourse did not last for at least twenty-seven minutes, then whole-body bioelectrical energies would not have sufficient time to be exchanged, no matter how many genital orgasms were produced. Hearing these words, Rudolph became angry, replying that he needed freedom and passion in his love life. To follow some set of rules—kiss eight minutes, embrace twelve minutes, lie touching twenty-seven minutes—would turn sex into some sort of military drill. Rudolph, who prided himself on being a wild, uninhibited, artistic lover, left angrily, saying that he would never follow Von Urban's advice. The doctor thought that there are primitive tribes that could teach Rudolph much in the art of passion.

Couples such as Rudolph and Mimi could never be called passionless. Their passion, however, is not based on full emotional intimacy and bodily surrender. Passionate, romantic love, thrives on obstacles, jealousies, partings, brief reconciliations, anxieties, fantasies, idealizations and fiction. In such love, emotion is often caught up in a game of reactive feelings, a logic of oppositions, offense and defense, conflict and warfare. Such "relationships" become a dual mirage, a mutual nonrelational dramatization of separateness, doubt, jealousy, and fear. As in chess, what are nurtured are loveless meditations, mazes of solitude, scores of illusory strategies toyed with and abandoned in succession, long labyrinths of thought relieved only by the intermittent and manipulative rearrangement or "capture" of the opponent. The acute sense of separation and doubt such love favors demands release through repetitive, passionate sex and orgasm—through a nonrelational, momentary, genitally localized oblivion that serves as a kind of fleeting sexual-political asylum. Such a couple does not know what it means to surrender and relax the entire body and heart in loving communion. Their deepest levels of sexual intimacy cannot unfold without the submission of their entire physical and emotional beings. They will tend only to manipulate each other like pawns in the game of their own private moment of release—for eroticism rather than true intimacy.

Fully developed sexuality and even spirituality are not self-absorbed, but require whole-body conductivity of emotional and vital energy. Relationship, communication, and commitment are the only cures for self-absorbed, manipulative erotic strategies. Therefore, lovers who wish to experience whole-body conductivity must be able not only to exchange their genital fluids, but mutually to yield and confess all their private, divisive tactics of isolation, erotic tendencies, and rituals. They should eliminate all taboos and play out their most private fantasies before each other. This in itself is the beginning of intimacy, for when all existing tendencies are yielded mutually, without guilt or criticism, to relaxed play, consideration, and inspection, full feeling can then develop and the energies that have been locked up in patterns of self-isolation and avoidance may circulate. If a couple persists in their openness, conventional orgasm as a means of release from feeling separate will become much less necessary. It will be replaced by the pleasure of prolonged, general, diffused conductivity of the life force, profound caring, and relational intensity.

Traditional Tantra in India skirts the problem of emotional reactivity by making strangers sexual partners. Then it is easy for lovers to imagine each other as forms of the God and the Goddess. However, this is a culture in which spiritual reality is primary and relationships on the human level are only secondary. The Tantric approach merely avoids the problem of relationship rather than solving it—for unless true emotional and bodily intimacy is brought to the test of committed day-to-day reality, it is, however divine it may seem, merely like going to church on Sundays.

India in general is a monument to an overemphasis on subjectivity, and in Tantra, one sees one's lover merely as a door to the celestial. There is nothing wrong with this as long as one also appreciates one's lover as a human being. Otherwise the entire relational self is not brought into play and the spiritual experience of Tantra becomes just another form of self-isolation and avoidance.

Since life is neither wholly inner nor wholly outer, fixating on either pole diminishes the fullness of life. Each pole, inner and outer, must be experienced. Lovers must transcend gross sexual activity in order to experience more delicate and unifying inner fields. Yet experiencing these inner levels must not become an end in itself, but must be transmuted into a relationship. Lovers must surrender both to infinity and to the demands of finite relatedness if their love is to be both spiritual and humanly authentic.

Traditional Tantra and Taoist teachings realized that conventional orgasm is not the goal of sexual intimacy. Rather, amplification and mutual sharing of bioelectrical and spiritual energies are valued. Both the Taoists and the Indians felt that the retention of sexual fluids gives vitality and augments health, longevity, and spirituality. Traditional Hindu medical treatises claim that it takes twenty-eight days for the male body to produce semen. During this period, digested food is transformed into lymph, blood, muscle, fat, bone, bone marrow, and finally semen. When conserved, the semen can be changed into subtle substances that flood the entire body with vitality and light. To shed semen excessively can cause weakness and lead to various illnesses. Many other religions, including Jewish Hasidism and Islamic Sufism, equate semen with vitality, light, and spirituality. In Homeric and post-Homeric Greece the psyche was thought to be contained in the head and spinal marrow. It was related to breath and believed to escape the body through the emission of semen.

Research published in 1981 by a team of sexologists found that women, too, are capable of ejaculation. The fluid that is emitted is produced in the area of the G spot, which is anatomically analogous to the prostate gland in men, and is similar to male ejaculatory fluid. It contains prostatic acid, phosphatase, and glucose. Both Tantric and Taoist traditions teach that women have more sexual fluid and vitality than men, yet advise that a woman can deplete her vitality through excessive orgasm. These traditions view excessive, conventional ejaculatory orgasm as degenerative for both sexes, therefore they developed styles of sexual intimacy that amplify and harmonize vital energies without expending them. In a contemplative embrace, the vital and emotional fields interweave and finally merge, causing an orgasm of the entire being that involves genital pleasure while transcending genital discharge. In this way sex serves a regenerative function, nourishing the entire nervous system.

Traditional Eastern approaches to sex, however, involve ritualistic and religious elements that are not appropriate to Western culture. The following guidelines, then, are for Western lovers who wish to explore the field approach to physical intimacy without exotic trappings. These guidelines should not be considered rules, but simply procedures for allowing physical intimacy to be an occasion for the contemplation of the flow of the life force rather than its manipulation and exploitation.

First of all, you and your lover should be emotionally prepared—for what you are in your feelings you will be sexually. Unitive energies will flow in an unrestricted manner to the degree that your emotional fountains will not be obstructed by anger, fear, jealousy, and doubt.

Next, you and your lover should be clean, not only for aesthetic reasons, but because bathing enhances the exchange of bioelectrical energies. Also, you should be relaxed and free of fatigue. If you are tense, then you will not fully feel the flow of vital energies, but instead will use the event to throw off tension via conventional orgasm. Surrender can only be an abstraction to tense muscles. Traditional cultures prescribe gentle stretching exercises, deep breathing, and meditation as preliminaries. Westerners, too, may want to sit with eyes closed and inhale with full feeling, letting the attention and breath bathe and dissolve any areas of unease. Imagine that you are taking in life energy during inhalation and breathing away tension during exhalation. You may want to massage one another, as this is also an effective means of freeing obstructed energies. Heavy oils, however, should not remain on the skin, as they will obstruct the exchange of bioelectrical currents.

If you meditate, it is best to do so before entering into an embrace, because it will increase your sensitivity to subtle energies. Alcohol and drugs should not be used, as they dull and distort the attention. For the same reason, it is best also not to eat a heavy meal beforehand. Several hours after mealtime, or in the morning after eating some fruit or tea, is better. This way the energy is not engaged in digestion and can circulate more freely.

Since this type of sexual union may last for several hours, it would be good to be in an environment that is free from intrusions. The telephone should be taken off the hook, and any children should be off at school or the movies. You will find it beneficial to do a few repetitions of the deer exercise, as described on pages 75 and 76. Combined with deep breathing, this exercise will awaken the sexual energies and diffuse them throughout the entire body.

Once you feel that your bodies are free of tension, you can begin kissing and caressing very slowly and easily. This will have the effect of stimulating bio-electrical, biochemical, and emotional streams. As these energies are aroused, they will begin to flow. If you are habituated to conventional sex, the energies will flow toward the genitals, where they will create a localized tension that seeks release through orgasm. Therefore, as these streams of energy begin building within you and your partner, you may want occasionally to discontinue kissing and caressing and surrender emotionally and bodily to the flow. This will diffuse the energy away from the genitals, thus relaxing the need for orgasm. The more you give in to these currents of energy, the more you will feel a deepening union.

Rather than favoring the excitement of genital tension and focusing on it, let the excitement flow freely and quietly through the entire body, breathing and relaxing into it continually. Remain in the present, enjoying and contemplating the relaxed warmth of nondemanding, full-body contact. Do not exploit your partner as a means to your own private satisfaction, but relax and submit to your growing vitality and emotion.

As the woman becomes moist, the sexual organs can gradually come into contact and then into full union. Penetration is not absolutely necessary for a complete merging of energies. What should be felt, more than the male penetrating the female physically, is a mutual interpenetration of sexual, emotional, and spiritual energies. If any fear is present, especially the fear of pregnancy, the woman will hold back emotionally and prevent the upward flow, circulation, and diffusion of energies.

If, however, no fear of pregnancy is present, and you and your partner feel like bringing your sexual organs into full union, you should do so very easily. The woman should slowly absorb her lover's penis into her vagina, and both should remember to breathe and relax into the wave of excitement that may accompany penetration.

Now that your sexual organs are in union, the moist vaginal walls in contact with the penis will act as a conduit for the intensified flow of vital energies. As waves of excitement rise within you, just let your lover be on the periphery of your awareness for a moment. Forget about sex and submit yourself to the flood of warmth. Merge into it. Remain centered in it, and then radiate this feeling to your lover. The submission, merging, and radiation will dissolve your hearts, liquify your beings, and make you feel as if you are falling through limitless space. You will experience an ecstasy in which you are totally one with your lover. Your breathing will become one, indeed, you may feel as if you are breathing inside each other. At times, your combined breathing may even become very refined and cease momentarily.

Only when the man feels that his erection is going to be lost, or when the woman feels a need for stimulation, should movement be necessary. Even then, let the waves of excitement build only so high, and instead of letting them crest and explode in orgasm, relax into their energy. Then you can remain in this embrace for hours without throwing off vital energy through conventional orgasm. You will be revitalizing each other by sinking deeper and deeper into softer and softer fields of radiant energy and emotion.

The technique, then, is not based on control. You are not seeking to avoid orgasm or to manipulate your bodily energies; you are merely closing your eyes, feeling those energies stream into your heart, head, and genitals and those of your lover, and allowing them to circulate, forming a contemplative circle of vitality. As your beings liquefy and merge, you may experience becoming luminous. But you are always relaxing, relaxing, falling back into the heart. Effortless awareness is the key. All your energies will be drawn upward, diffused throughout the body, and absorbed into increasingly more exalted energy centers. As this takes place, lustful tendencies will be transmuted into feelings of love and the need for conventional orgasm will lessen.

After embracing this way for about thirty-five minutes, you may begin to experience wave after wave of orgasmic sensations throughout your entire being. If you are male, you will not ejaculate, but your entire body, along with your lover's, will suddenly feel a subtle shuddering or trembling that is not localized at the sexual center. Your bodies may begin to shake spontaneously. Do not remain detached, but enter the shaking, become it, knowing that two bodily energies are merging completely. The trembling will probably not last long, and afterward you will feel deeply relaxed, vital, and radiant. It is important at this point to remain united easily with your lover for at least a half an hour after the trembling. A feeling of aliveness will last for hours, or even days, and you will probably feel no need to repeat intercourse for a while.

To summarize, in order to experience the full depth of the field approach to sex, it is necessary to play-fully and nondemandingly kiss and caress each other for at least a half-hour beforehand. This allows the energies to awaken and grow. Then you should lie together, motionlessly, with full and relaxed atten-tion and with your sexual organs either joined or in close physical proximity. This embrace may last for hours. If your bodies begin to tremble, allow it to happen, and then remain in an embrace for at least another half-hour.

During the first few weeks or months, one or both partners may feel a tendency toward conventional or-gasm. This can cause various situations. It may hap-pen that just by lying motionless with his partner, the male may ejaculate or his partner may experience or-gasm. If this should occur, just allow it to happen ef-fortlessly. It is a result of previous sexual habits. Be certain, however, to remain together in a restful, mo-tionless embrace for at least a half-hour after the or-gasm.

A second situation may arise in which no orgasm takes place spontaneously, but a great deal of tension is felt in the genitals. If this persists even after you and your partner have remained in a motionless em-brace for at least a half-hour, consider that time a prel-ude to conventional intercourse and orgasm, which you can then enjoy. Intercourse can be prolonged by following a simple procedure. As either partner ap-proaches orgasm, cease all movement, breathe deeply, and relax into the energy and emotion—into the heart. At this moment you can perform a few cycles of the deer exercise and feel the sexual energy, which has been accumulating in the genital region, spread to the heart, throat, head, limbs—and to your lover. *The deer exercise should never be performed during orgasm.*

As always, after conventional intercourse and orgasm, you should lie together fully relaxed with your sexual organs in close contact for at least a half-hour. Otherwise the full exchange of bioelectrical energies will not take place and you may feel the need to repeat the act. After a few weeks, as your bodies become more relaxed in love, the tendency toward genital tension will lessen.

In a third situation, you and your lover may feel little or no urge toward orgasm, but may simply feel bored or that you are missing something without the excitement of stimulation and orgasmic release. Again, this feeling is because of habit and will not persist for long. In all these cases, you should not feel that you have failed, it is just that your habits have not yet been transformed. It is important to remember that there is nothing specific that *should* happen. You and your lover are merely allowing a field of relaxed energy and emotion to develop between you. Finally, your bodies will become accustomed to the accumulated energies. An augmented sense of health, strength, vitality, and clarity of mind will be felt. Full sexual communion is not primarily a matter of technique, performance, control, avoidance of orgasm or manipulation and exploitation of your own or your partner's energies. It concerns emotional and bodily relaxation, surrender, submission, and absorption. There is really nothing that must be done; the way to do is to be. Nevertheless, there are some techniques that can be applied in the beginning to help rechannel the energies in the direction of the heart and higher energy centers. These include periodic use of the deer exercise before and during intercourse, and full, relaxed breathing with an awareness of the sexual energy spreading throughout your entire body.

Since this type of intimacy may last for many hours, the most suitable positions are ones that afford maximum comfort to both partners. You can experiment with various embraces, though most Western lovers are not flexible enough to assume most of the positions indicated in Eastern texts. One of the most relaxing is as follows:

The lovers recline on a bed at right angles to each other. Their upper bodies are away from each other, and their pelvic regions are in contact. The woman rests on her back while the man is on his right side. Their legs are intertwined, with the man's left leg between the woman's legs; her left leg rests atop his left hip. They may lie together motionless like this for a half-hour or more as they contemplate the energies flowing between them. Then the man can penetrate the woman, remaining in this position for at least another half-hour. Remember, if ejaculation occurs before the half-hour period is up, the lovers should remain in the position for at least another half-hour so that their energies may become fully equalized.

Couples should not think just because ejaculation does not occur during this type of embrace that they can forget about birth control. If even one drop of semen seeps out, it is sufficient to cause conception. Therefore, couples wishing to avoid pregnancy should use a reliable method of birth control. However, barrier methods of birth control such as condoms and diaphragms inhibit somewhat the free flow of bioelectrical energies. Therefore, the couple should decide upon a method that will allow maximum psychological ease and minimum bioelectrical disruption.

Lovers new to this approach may feel that they are missing something at first, that an element has been left out. They would do well to remember that Hemingway's sparse prose style, the starkly etched musical improvisations of Thelonious Monk, and the luminous vacuities of Chinese landscape painting all achieve power through silence, non-doing, and emptiness. Or take as an example the vacuum state of a particle as described in quantum physics. The particle itself is nothing but an excitation of its inactive field. This vacuum field actually does nothing, yet it contains simultaneously all possible excited states— all particulate forms. The emptiness is a fullness. Then there is the God Shiva, sitting in meditation and enjoying simultaneously the bliss of 186,000,000 sexual postures, or the God incarnate Krishna, who symbolizes the same quiet inner fullness, making love with scores of cowherd women simultaneously in sixteen postures. This may help explain why some yogis, even though celibate, have such enormous grins.

Notes

1. Harold Robbins, *The Betsy* (New York: Pocket Books, 1971), pp. 101–3.
2. Shere Hite, *The Hite Report* (New York: Macmillan, 1976), pp. 385–86.
3. Ibid., p. 386.
4. Ibid., p. 387.
5. Ibid., p. 387.
6. Ibid., p. 385.
7. Burton Watson, trans. *The Complete Works of Chuang Tzu* (New York: Columbia University Press, 1978), pp. 200–10.
8. I have followed the translation of Cornelia Dimmitt and J.A.B. van Buitenen, *Classical Hindu Mythology* (Philadelphia: Temple University Press, 1978), pp. 258–262.
9. Gopi Krishna, *Kundalini* (Berkeley, Cal.: Shambala Publications, 1970), pp. 11–13.
10. Alice Stockham, *Karezza: Ethics of Marriage* (R. F. Fenno and Company, 1903), pp. 26–27.

Index